LET THE *Morning* BRING ME WORD

Linda Wasson

Artwork by Peyton Schmidt

ISBN 979-8-88540-656-7 (paperback)
ISBN 979-8-88540-657-4 (digital)

Copyright © 2022 by Linda Wasson

All rights reserved. No part of this publication may be reproduced, distributed, or transmitted in any form or by any means, including photocopying, recording, or other electronic or mechanical methods without the prior written permission of the publisher. For permission requests, solicit the publisher via the address below.

Christian Faith Publishing
832 Park Avenue
Meadville, PA 16335
www.christianfaithpublishing.com

Printed in the United States of America

*To my great aunt Bessie Johnson—
writer and prayer warrior, whose prayers
have echoed throughout our family,
like ripples on a pond.*

*To my uncle Gene Burgan—
writer and family historian
and my namesake.*

*To my children and grandchildren—
to a thousand generations,
as the Lord has promised to all who love him.*

*To the one who sees us,
knows us,
and loves us,
the author and perfecter of our faith—
Our great God and savior,
Jesus Christ.*

Do not be afraid, for you will not be put to shame;
Don't be humiliated, for you will not be disgraced.
For you will forget the shame of your youth,
And you will no longer remember the disgrace of your widowhood.
Indeed, your husband is your Maker, His name is "Yahweh of Hosts"—
And the Holy One of Israel is your Redeemer,
He is called the God of all the earth.
For the Lord has called you, like a wife deserted and wounded
in spirit, a wife of one's youth when she is rejected, says your God.
"I deserted you for a brief moment, but I will take you back
with great compassion. In a surge of anger, I hid my face from
you for a moment, but I will have compassion on you
with everlasting love," says the Lord your Redeemer—
My love will not be removed from you and My covenant
of peace will not be shaken, says your compassionate Lord—
Then all your children will be taught by the
Lord, their prosperity will be great,
and you will be established on a foundation of righteousness.
You will be far from oppression, you will certainly not be afraid;
You will be far from terror, it will certainly not come near you.
If anyone attacks you, it is not from Me;
Whoever attacks you will fall before you.
Look, I have created the craftsman who blows on the
charcoal fire and produces a weapon suitable for its task;
—no weapon formed against you will succeed,
and you will refute any accusation raised against you in court.
This is the heritage of the Lord's servants, and
their righteousness is from Me,
This is the Lord's declaration.

—Isaiah 54:4–17 HCSB

Preface

Psalm 143:8 (NIV) reads, "Let the morning bring me word of your unfailing love, for I have put my trust in you."

I have a large plaque, hanging in my library. Though it was purchased several years ago, its meaning still stirs and deeply pierces my heart. It is a message. I can't help but think you have heard it too. It captured my attention so long ago, but I have been waiting—waiting to hear—listening.

It is hard to quell the thoughts that unceasingly flood my mind. Silencing my mouth is one thing—my mind is another. My mind was not made that way.

My mind and heart were created to search. They are always listening, always restless, always hoping, always looking. Are there even words to express this? I am not sure.

The plaque reads, "Let us be silent that we may hear the whisper of God."

Did you hear that? I will say it again—the whisper of God!

Not my own imagination, not the voice of others—nothing else will do.

His voice is speaking to me—his heart of love for me. I have only just realized how much I need to hear from him—more than I can say, more than I have realized in the past or known how to express to others.

I need this. I need to hear his voice.

The psalmist understood, as he cried out in Psalm 63:1 (HCSB), "I eagerly seek You. I thirst for You; my body faints for You," and again in Psalm 73:25–26, 28 (ESV):

> Whom have I in heaven but you? And there is nothing on earth that I desire besides you. My flesh and my heart may fail, but God is the strength of my heart and my portion forever—but as for me it is good to be near God; I have made the Lord God my refuge.

If I am quiet, I hear his whispers deep within me. I see him everywhere. His love surrounds me. I cannot escape it, nor do I want to—ever!

Could it really be that the deepest needs of our hearts were placed there by him so that the world could never satisfy and we would search for him? We don't just imagine those needs, nor did he cruelly place them there to torment us. Could it be that the deepest, most secret longings in our hearts were placed there by him so that he could reveal to us his unfathomable love—to do for us what only he could ever do or bring to pass?

Maybe our greatest failure is to settle for less than what his heart is longing to give.

I used to be happy when I heard from God once and awhile. This is no longer true.

Like the Canaanite woman who came crying out for mercy and begging Jesus to heal her daughter, she responded by saying, "Even the dogs eat from the crumbs that fall from their master's table" (Matthew 15:27 ESV). I have been satisfied with crumbs on the floor, when he has been calling me to his banquet table.

"For His banner over me is love. I am my beloved's, and his desire is toward me" (Song of Solomon 2:4, 7:10 KJV).

Do you know that you don't have to beg God to love you? He just does.

Let's turn down the volume of the world and listen. We will hear him call our name and know that his love knows no measure. We will not need to beg him for crumbs of acceptance.

There is nothing we can do to earn his attention. His eyes have been fixed upon us since eternity.

He had a plan to send us the help we needed.

He sent his only beloved Son, Jesus Christ to reconcile us and to take the punishment we deserve. He gave his Son because we are his treasure, his chosen, his beloved!

Let us be silent that we may hear the whisper of God.

Introduction

I was sixteen years old the day the teacher posed the question to our English class. No one had ever asked me that question, and it took me by surprise—as I assume it did most of the thirty or so other kids in the room that day. Even if I had known the answer, I would not have raised my hand, as the world I lived in was very much in the privacy of my own mind. I couldn't have spoken, even if I had an answer. I didn't. There was silence in the room. Everyone waited. The teacher waited.

Finally, one brave hand went up slowly, and we all looked her way.

"So why do you exist? What is your purpose?" the teacher challenged her.

I knew her to be a Christian and wasn't surprised to hear her answer—"to know God." There was more silence in the room, and as though no one had answered the question, the teacher changed the subject and continued on in another direction.

That was fifty-four years ago, and I still remember that day.

If I had been forced to search my heart, the only answer that would have risen to the surface would have, could have been, "to be loved."

In that same class, I was fascinated by a poem written by Robert Frost. You know, the one titled "A Road Not Taken."

> Two roads diverged in a yellow wood,
> And sorry I could not travel both
> And be one traveler, long I stood

And looked down one as far as I could
To where it bent in the undergrowth;
Then took the other, as just as fair,
And having perhaps the better claim,
Because it was grassy and wanted wear;
Though as for the passing there
Had worn them really about the same,
And both that morning equally lay
In leaves no step had trodden black.
Oh! I kept the first for another day!
Yet knowing how way leads on to way,
I doubted if I should ever come back.
I shall be telling this with a sigh
Somewhere ages and ages hence;
Two roads diverged in a wood, and I—
I took the one less traveled by,
And that has made all the difference.

My heart was strangely attracted to this idea of taking the lesser trodden path, yet in my fears, I still chose to take the first, and I married two years later.

There are no regrets—yet, I now know that the less traveled path was the path I was called to journey on through life. Somehow that was where I ended up, despite my early choosing.

Chapter 1

There were many things, back then, that I did not understand and many things I had yet to learn. There were things that were too big for my young heart.

Jeremiah 1:5a reads, "Before I formed you in the womb I knew you" (ESV).

The day I was born, my mother told me that I was in a hurry to get into the world (I have no memory of that). Back in those days, mothers went through labor and delivery without pain meds and without the knowledge of the child's sex or the ability to choose which day their children were to be born. That was the way it was. The second child of three, I arrived.

We lived in a small house my father had built by himself out in the country in Osseo, Minnesota.

My earliest memories are happy and carefree—wandering in the fields, searching for wild strawberries, climbing trees, looking for bird's nests, and walking to church a mile down a dirt country road. Mom had friends all the way down the road and would frequently stop and visit.

I was so bored. She needed to talk, and as an introvert, I didn't. I had other things to do.

She was lonely and needed friends—my young heart was on an adventure.

Around the age of twenty-four, she had accepted Jesus as her savior and eagerly told everyone she could get to listen to her, about their need for forgiveness and God's love. Her bluntness turned many off, but she tried.

My father was not in the least bit interested or impressed with her newfound faith.

As for my brother or sister, I have no memories, except for my brother frightening me with stories about a man who was in the tiny, small room that my grandfather would sleep in when he visited. I never once opened that door and peaked in—never.

My dad would shoot his bow and arrows in the field, and I remember him chopping off the head of chickens and them flopping around, squirting blood everywhere. *Uck*!

My mom made the best of things and hung out the laundry to dry, even in the winter. The clothes would be frozen, as she brought them inside.

We were poor, but somehow, my mom found nice little dresses for us girls.

My grandfather would stop every year and take a picture of us. I cherish those pictures. They have given me a record of my childhood.

One Christmas, I sang "Away in the Manger" at church. My mom was so proud. Interestingly, it is my favorite childhood song.

> Away in a manger, no crib for a bed. The little Lord Jesus laid down his sweet head.
>
> The stars in the bright sky looked down where he lay. The little Lord Jesus asleep on the hay.
>
> The cattle are lowing, the baby awakes, but little Lord Jesus no crying he makes
>
> I love you Lord Jesus, look down from the sky and stay by my cradle till morning is nigh.
>
> Be near me Lord Jesus, I ask Thee to stay close by me forever and love me I pray.
>
> Bless all the dear children in Thy tender care and fit us for Heaven to live with Thee there.

Do you hear that? *Be near me, Lord Jesus—I ask thee to stay close by me forever.*

That has never left me.

I didn't know then that he knew me. I didn't know then that he was watching over me with great care. I didn't know then that he not only knew my name but that he was whispering it, he was calling me. I couldn't hear him, but that didn't matter at that point. He was.

Many years later, he would show me that the very day I was born, he was there. He was rejoicing that his daughter had been born. That day, I became a Daddy's girl.

That was one of the things I had yet to learn.

Chapter 2

Isaiah 46:3–4 (ESV) reads, "Listen to me, [you] who have been borne [sustained] by me from before your birth, carried from the womb, I have made [you], and I will bear [you]; I will carry [you] and I will save [you]."

I can't say I heard God's voice back in my very early years, but maybe, he was speaking to my heart as I ran freely through the fields filled with wonder at nature, in love with solitude, adventure, and with a clear awareness of all that was around me. It was a sweet time.

He was and is smiling. I know this now. I didn't then.

I am amazed at all the memories a six-year-old can gather, and I wonder about what memories my own children have secretly stored from their very young years.

I guess that would be their stories—my hope would be that they would discover that the God who created them in my womb has written his story upon their hearts as well. They have a purpose and are deeply cherished by me and by God.

We lived on a dirt road that ended in a cornfield. I marvel that we were given the freedom to explore anything on that road. I got to know all of the other six families that lived there at the time. There was a family with a girl my age who lived in (probably) the original old farmhouse.

The Bartons lived across the street with a son my brother's age, a wealthy family who didn't let other children inside their home—a poor, dirty family with lots of kids and a mother who was always nursing a baby, an old couple, who were my dad's friends, and a nice family with a girl my age. They had geese running in their yard, which I was deathly afraid of. But I would venture there because they also had a small aquarium with fish that I was fascinated by. Like, who has something that wonderful in their home? We didn't have even a bathroom, and my parents slept in the living room on a couch bed. We kids had the only bedroom with a single twin bed for my brother and two cribs for my sister and me. The toilet was in the corner between the cribs. There were no walls around it. I remember peeking over the end of the crib one time while my grandfather was sitting there. Needless to say, that event did not endear me to him, and he was quite upset! I guess that I did have a little bit of stinker in my heart!

Starting school put me into a big world of people unknown to me and away from the safety of home. I was eager to learn but easily embarrassed. I remember taking a test and not knowing that bananas have black seeds. That was my first moment of being aware of shame. That winter, the school flooded an area for a skating rink and roped it off until it was thoroughly frozen. That morning, my brother encouraged me to go out and walk on it. Of course, I couldn't read the sign that told you not to, and I fell down. I got my clothes all soaking wet. The only extra clothes my kindergarten teacher had were pants and a T-shirt. Girls never wore anything but dresses back then, and I was, for a second time, deeply embarrassed. A brother should take care of his sisters.

It was an early lesson. I remember learning to read in first grade with Dick and Jane. It was hard to me.

Then came the day—the fateful day!

We had to walk half a block up the dirt road to catch the bus.

One fall day, I remember so clearly, as we got off the school bus, that there were a whole bunch of cars down the road at our home. I said to myself, "Oh! We have company!" I was so excited because it was not normal to have any company.

As I walked down the road, to my surprise, our home was gone. It had burned to the ground. There was nothing but ashes. Nothing! Everything I had was gone!

I learned later that my mom had rescued a few things—all the photographs, a pair of glass candlesticks (a wedding gift from my father's parents), our baby books, and my teddy bear (a gift from my grandmother for my first Christmas). I still have all of these things.

My mother never talked about it then, but apparently, she was at the neighbors and saw the fire. She ran inside and grabbed these things before the fire got too big.

The Salvation Army gave us food and clothes, which was kind of them.

The story was later told. My mom's version was that an electrical shortage started the fire. My dad's version was that my mom had left the stove on, and it was her fault. I have always wanted to believe my dad.

I didn't know the truth until years later when I looked clearly at my childhood and God whispered to me, "If your mom started the fire in the kitchen, she would have never been able to get into the house to pull the things out, which she did." The only doorway into the house was in the kitchen. The fire couldn't possibly have started there. If I didn't have these things in my possession, I would have never known the truth.

But I do have them. Not that it matters much but it does to the extent that God wanted me to know that he saw me as a small child. His love can be found in the most unusual places. He wanted me to know that even in the tragic moments of our lives—in loss, in fire, in the storm—he is there. His love knows no boundaries or time—and in our weakness and helplessness, he is lovingly whispering, "Don't be afraid. I am here. I was there. I will always be with you."

I didn't know these things then, but I know them now. It creates a foundation that cannot be shaken, for many more storms would come my way.

So life started again as we moved into Minneapolis, just off of Central Avenue onto Quincy Street. A new chapter started, which wasn't quite so sunny, yet my heart was still on an adventure, and I was going to see what I could find. And off my little six-year-old heart went!

Chapter 3

Psalm 31:15 reads, "My times are in your hand" (ESV).

Moving from six acres out in the countryside to living in Minneapolis in a second-story apartment was a drastic change, yet I took it in stride.

We now had two bedrooms, a living room, and a larger kitchen—and a bathroom with a bathtub! We three kids still had one bedroom, and my brother's need to frighten us shifted to our closet and underneath my sister's and my bed. Somehow I still believed him, and my fears grew, along with fears of fires and loss and a general wonder about the future.

Maybe life was not as safe as when my little heart had danced unencumbered in the fields. I still had a great need to climb on things, of which my mother foresaw, and I was strictly warned not to climb on the white picket fence, separating our home from the neighbor's.

I was told to keep my climbing to the small metal swing set. It was too much for me, and one day (as the fence was right there next to the swing set), I slipped over and proceeded my balancing act with glee until I slipped and not only tore my pants but cut my leg. I had a great fear of being naughty and some pride, so I managed to dispose of the pants and hide my wound from my mom. She didn't always pay attention, and if she ever knew what I had done, it was never spoken about. It was my secret, and I would have never told my siblings.

School was no longer a bus ride but, rather, a six-block walk, which included traveling underneath several railroad bridges. This opened up the new opportunity for my brother to torment me. Now I had to watch for something called hobos and bums, who lived around the railroad tracks and waited to snatch little girls. They would just disappear and never be found again. Somehow, my mother joined into this story also. So I was banned from walking on the back side of the block.

I still needed to walk under the bridges every day on my way to and from school. My mom thought that being with my brother would somehow protect me. She learned soon enough that my brother was not the protector she had assumed, and as he bullied some other boys, they took it out on me.

Because of this, the next school year, Mom put us into a very small Christian school. I liked this little school, where my class had first, second, and third grades together. The teacher was very kind and she taught us the song "Children of the Heavenly Father." I loved this song and have never forgotten it. She also sang it to us in Swedish.

Then one day, she announced that it was her birthday. We clapped and wanted to sing "Happy Birthday" to her when she stopped us and told us that it wasn't the day she was born as a baby but, rather, when she had some second birth and came to know Jesus. I wondered about that. What did that mean?

My brother's continuous torment moved to the basement of that schoolhouse, to a closet at the end of the hallway. If you were disobedient, the punishment was sitting on the bottom of the stairs for a short period. I would assume that was how my brother discovered this new source of amusement.

My sister later told me the story of one night at the supper table—she didn't want to eat some kind of vegetables. She was mad at my mom for trying to force her. (We had to always clean our plates because there were starving children in Africa or something.) As I got older, I would slip things like liver to our dog. Anyways, my sister, who could not have been more than four or five at that time, was angry at my mom, so that night, when we were put into the bathtub together, she got some kind of cutting object and cut off some of my hair. I guess my mom wasn't happy.

Hair grows back, but somehow, there was some sibling stuff growing as well. My mother loved to curl our hair into banana curls.

We did not know my maternal grandmother much during our younger years. I will tell you of her story later when I share about my mom. But on my seventh birthday, she appeared at our home with the only birthday gift she would ever give me or any of us kids for that matter. It was a little, red leather Bible with my name inscribed in gold letters—Linda Jean Burgan. As an adult, I have come to realize the preciousness of this gift to me. It was prophetic, as God knew how much I would come to love his holy Word. I have to say that this little, red Bible, along with my teddy bear pulled from our house fire, are clear footprints to me of God's presence in my young life.

The heart of God is always carefully watching over his children—writing his story on their hearts. He wants us to recognize and find deep comfort in knowing that he has always been part of our story.

Psalm 139:13b, 16 (NASB) reads, "You wove me in my mother's womb, and in Your book were written all the days that were ordained for me, when as yet there were none of them.

The little, red Bible was a clear message from his heart to mine.

The summer I turned eight, my dad lost his job in Minneapolis, and he moved us down to Illinois, close to his parents and siblings. Now my life included family I had known nothing about.

Chapter 4

Children of the heavenly Father
Safely in his bosom gather
Nestling bird nor star in heaven
Such a refuge ere was given

Dad moved us down to Waukegan, Illinois, into a housing project of several thousand homes.

They were like cookie-cutter houses—all from the same floor plan. Some of them were two-bedroom, but most were three. Our new home had three bedrooms with 864 square feet. It would be my home until I married at age eighteen.

It is amazing the things you remember from your childhood.

Our address was 1649 Fraizer Street, and our phone number MA3-1528. My memories of the next six years are many, and as I went about in my own little world, I was still quite content. These years were filled with school, making friends in the neighborhood, having a paper route (though I have no memory of ever making money), but once a year, we were treated with going to a movie theater and having popcorn, which was a sin, yet my mom let me go. Maybe that was why I delivered papers. I also just loved to roller skate, which was my only real activity in those years. My last memory was of going to church.

In third grade, I had a boyfriend, who I liked for a very short time, until he pulled on my brand-new raincoat and ripped it. Having anything new was very special to me, and the damage to my new coat left me angry at him. I needed to walk the six blocks to school every day, and on the rainy days, it was a matter of staying dry. My mother did not drive until I became an adult, and my father was rarely home. So rain, shine, snow, and wind, we were on our own.

I am sure that I walked with my siblings at least some of the times, but as no one in our family talked much, I have little memories of that. I have almost no memories of any real relationship with either my brother or sister. I certainly can't say that was any of our fault. We were all introverts and accustomed to not speaking much to each other. My brother and sister would have to tell their own stories, as I have learned that people remember things differently. Personalities differ, birth order matters, personal encounters with others, and many other things form the way people view and respond to life. Some chose to see life either as a cup half full or half empty. I chose full, even in my younger years.

Today my cup is not only full, it is running over—but that is part of my story for later. All this is to say I do have a few memories of my siblings, and I do mean a few. I remember my brother forcing my little sister into the basement and shutting her down there. We were *both* terrified of the basement, and he tormented her many times. For some reason, he did not do that to me, but I had no power to stop him from frightening her. I now wish that I could have stopped him, as I understood the fear.

As for my sister, she was always spunky, which I didn't understand. I just wanted to live happily in my own little world and avoiding problems as much as possible—and look for adventure. My only real memory of my sister back then was that every few months, for some unknown reason to me, she wanted to fight me. She would swing her fists at me, and I would hold her back so she couldn't reach me. That made her madder, and she would end up crying and walking away. But she would come back again, six months or so later and try again. My last memory of this was when I was fourteen, which made her eleven or twelve. There was a reason that it stopped at that point, but we will talk about this coming up.

I had a dog named Sugar. I got her one day, walking home from school. There, sitting on a front-door step, was this little white puppy with black spots on her head. I went up to pet the pup, and a man who lived there came out and asked me if I wanted the dog. That day, I brought her home, and Mom didn't seem to mind—so I had a dog!

She eventually had two litters of puppies. Her second litter produced our next dog named Susie. She had a brother named Georgie, which I wanted to keep, but Mom was against boy dogs for some reason, so Susie, it was. We had to get rid of Sugar because she started to bite other people. Maybe kids teased her. I have no idea what Mom and Dad did with Sugar. I would guess one of my father's bullets found her.

Susie was a wonderful dog and kept my mom company for at least twenty years.

We were poor. I later learned that my dad would carry several uncashed checks in his wallet. My mom was given $25 a week, from my dad, to buy groceries. Eventually, my mom started babysitting other children to earn extra money. Only one time in those years did we ever have store-bought clothes. Our clothes came from two different ways.

Mom would take the public bus downtown to what was then the Goodwill. It was not like it is today. There would be long tables set out with piles and piles of clothing on top of them. Nothing was sorted into girls, boys, child, adult, or much less sizes. I was bored out of my mind as I waited for hours for her to hand sort through the piles and piles of clothing to find things that would fit us. So our first source of clothing was used hand-me-downs from the Goodwill. There were no such things as garage sales back then. Most people I knew didn't have a garage.

The second source was Mom sewing our dresses. It was awful fabric, and though her sewing was adequate, I was not too happy about it. She would make look-alike outfits for my sister and me. My sister had it the worst because she had to endure all of my leftover clothing, which I had outgrown. She also inherited my mom's poorer eye sight and had to wear outrageously ugly glasses. I do not know if these things were the source of my sister's anger, only she would really know, and she learned to hide behind walls she erected.

But back to my mom. As an adult, I realized that she was trying to do her best for us back then. I see her love. I see her struggles to make do with what she had. She tried.

Back in those years, I had what would be called today night terrors. I would have repetitive dreams when I was sick and wake up in the night unable to move or call out to my mom. It was a problem for me. Fear was a major struggle. I was all alone and didn't know how to stop this unseen enemy that creeped around in the darkness.

But on the lighter side, I loved the holidays. We always got together at my aunt Rose Mary and uncle Dennis's home. It was an exciting time to me. The most important thing was that, when we arrived, my aunt Rose Mary would hug me and she seemed so very happy to see me. She did that to everyone, but I didn't care. She hugged me. I will always remember and thank her for that. She is the only one I ever remember hugging me in those younger years. It meant something to me—something important. She also had fun with life. She had raccoons for pets and horses and a big house with a canopy bed. She always seemed happy. I envied her kids yet still enjoyed my moments there. They are good memories.

As I write this today, she is the last one of the aunts and uncles living. My hope is that I can finish this before she is gone. I will always love my aunts—not only her but the others I learned to love and cherish later.

Aunts are very important to little girls—very important. I learned that from experience. I suppose this is the best time to talk about the wider family.

As I have mentioned earlier, my maternal grandmother was pretty much unseen in my earlier years. She had shown up in Minneapolis back on my seventh birthday and gave me my little, red Bible. I don't recall seeing her again until I was an adult. I had no good or bad feelings about her. Later, when I was older, she moved to Grand Rapids, and my mom's brother, Bob, build her a home next to him on Pokegama Lake after her last husband died. She had four. Did I inherit that?

At that point, I enjoyed going up to visit her. One time, I took my guitar up and played for her. She seemed to enjoyed that. I loved it that she had French doors in her living room that went out to her porch. I loved them, and I wished that, someday, I could have them too. God knew my heart, so out of love for me, I have French doors in the library of the home I later bought. I remember my grandmother and see the precious love of God, my Father.

One more thing about my grandmother, Eleanor—on one visit to her home, I noticed that she had beautiful China with pretty blue flowers. I told her how lovely they were. When she passed away in 1989, I was astonished to find that she had left them to me in her will. I have them to this day, as a final gift of love from her.

As for my maternal grandfather, he lived up in Grand Rapids in the spring and summer. Then he drove down to Texas for the winters. He told us that he had visited every state except Hawaii. That was so amazing to me that he had traveled so much!

He loved to travel. I do too! He would take our pictures on his way through, and I will be ever grateful to him for that gift. I cherish them. He had a heart attack around the age of fifty, and my mother told me that was when he became a Christian. I think my mom had prayed for him, but that is only my assumption. He would bring games with him, and he played them with us. I remember Rack-O the most. He also brought candy, which was rare to us, and I loved it. But I grew to have hard feelings toward him because he was a very nervous type of person and he would tell us that we were going to give him another heart attack. Somehow, he made it clear that we were not nice children. As a child, that offended me and did not leave loving thoughts in my heart toward him. He would also tell us that the children in Texas loved him more than we did. Maybe they did. Maybe his words impacted me because of my paternal grandfather.

Our move to Illinois brought him into our lives. He did not like my mother and, as a result, strongly disliked us. He never said one kind word to us and clearly disliked us being at his home. All I ever saw of him was sitting in his chair, watching baseball and smoking cigarettes.

I had a grandfather who hated me and one who thought I was going to give him a heart attack. That is a lot for a little girl. I had lessons to learn about forgiveness.

I thought that there was something wrong with me. To say that it took me a long time to figure that one out would be longer than I would like to say. I felt like a worse person when, at the age around ten, he died of cancer—and I was happy he was gone. There was something wrong with me. Seriously, wrong with me!

Now my paternal grandmother was a sweetheart. She was very quiet, and I don't even remember if we ever really talked, but she would make this wonderful homemade bread, which I loved. She always had a bird in a cage for a pet. But best of all, I remember the beautiful flower garden that she had. It was the best, and I think that I started gardening later in life because of my grandmother. I loved her the best in my own quiet way.

These people are who I came from.

I had cousins too, but as I was the third oldest, my memories of them were mostly about my cousin Debbie. We hung out for a while until my family broke apart. She passed away many years ago at a young age. I also had two male cousins from my mom's brother. They lived in northern Minnesota.

Finally, I would like to share about going to church as a young girl. We were Baptists.

Most of the years, we attended church three times a week. I have a lot to say about this, as it was probably the most impactful influence in my life. I didn't understand all of this back then, and my views are from looking back and trying to remember the best that I can. I remember being taught to be a good girl, which I tried to do. I thought that being a Christian *was* being good. We always brought our Bibles to church.

I learned the words to the hymns. I memorized the books of the Bible before third grade was over, and as the years went by, I could beat almost everyone in my class at finding scriptures in what they called sword drills with my little, red Bible. I also found that, somehow, it was easy to memorize scripture verses. So at their awards night, they always had me lead as we quoted out loud the verses we had learned. I could say the words perfect, and I guess I had a loud voice. I learned a hundred if I learned one.

I made my mother proud. That made me feel loved. I am sure that the leaders thought that they had done a rewarding job. I do thank them for the time that they had spent and pray that they will be rewarded.

We were always told that we needed to have a personal relationship with Jesus. Several times during those years, I prayed their prayer quietly in my heart to give my heart to Jesus. But it just seemed like words, and nothing seemed to happen. So I believed them and thought that was all that happened when you became a Christian.

My dad would always pick us up from church at least half an hour late. We were always the last ones in the parking lot. He was very much against believing in God. I was always a daddy's girl—always. I wanted very much for him to love me. I pursued that for many years until the day he died.

But that is getting off on a rabbit trail, and I want to finish.

When I prayed this prayer as a child, I repeated words. There was no real repentance and turning from my sins in my heart. I also prayed this prayer because I didn't want to go to hell.

I remember having thoughts (which I now know were from the deceiver, the devil) that if I gave my whole heart to God, he would force me to be a missionary. I didn't want to be a missionary, and I couldn't tell God I would do something and not do it. I also believed that he would take away everything that I loved, including my family. I was a little girl, and I believed these whispers. I didn't know what truth was, and as an introvert, I would have never asked about these things. I just wanted to avoid all problems in life as much as I could.

I thought that what I had was all being a Christian was. I know now that God was quietly whispering my name. I know now that God was patiently and lovingly watching over me and guarding me as his very own child, though I had not yet discovered the truth of all these things. These are a few of the things I remember from those innocent six years in Illinois.

Little did I know that things were going to change quite quickly, and I was not ready for them. Neither did my years in church give me the light or help that I would need in those dark times ahead. Soon, I would really be all alone, or at least that was how I felt, even if it was not true at all. Sometimes, in the dark places of our lives, we find ourselves very lost—but even that is a really good thing. It is important that we learn how lost we really are without God.

Chapter 5

Romans 3:23 reads, "For all have sinned and fall short of the glory of God" (ESV).

I was wakened by loud sobbing. My mother was on the telephone directly below my bedroom, hysterically crying to a friend. I was fourteen and a half and a freshman in high school. I had no idea why she was crying or that whatever was happening that morning would affect me the rest of my life. In my selfishness, there was irritation welling up in me at the disturbance below.

My parents had never fought in a manner that I was aware of—no yelling, arguing, or outward signs of problems. I had never lived with alcohol addiction or abuse or anything serious other than no one in our family talked to one another and there was little emotional affection. Dad thought that emotions were for weak people and he wasn't weak. All of this put a serious roadblock to the reality of our emotional needs. In his opinion, only weak people needed God as a crutch, and he was not one of them.

This noise that my mom was making was breaking into my little world, and I didn't like it one bit. I feared problems and wanted no part of them. I avoided them at all cost. I had no clue what to do with them. I had never learned that. Avoidance at all cost was the road I would take for many years until I learned that avoidance only gave a problem time to grow larger. But for now, my mother was sobbing and sobbing and sobbing and sobbing. She wouldn't stop and I became seriously angry at her.

There was no escaping from the tears. I would later take it on as my responsibility to fix. Sometime in there, my brother ran away from home and was gone for a year. I have no clear memory of when that happened; only he could say. Later, my sister would run away also and unlike my brother, she never came back. She found refuge at my dad and his girlfriend's home. She would be the only one my father ever spent any time actually being a dad to. My lifelong feelings were that Dad never really had any desire to be a father. Where did that leave a child?

So for months, my mom cried—actually, it went on for at least ten years. Somewhere in there, we switched roles. It became my job. I became the mother, and she became the daughter. Maybe I took that on myself, but Mom seemed to need it, and I volunteered. My dad left her for a woman he met at work, and this second major rejection in her life was more than she could manage to handle.

Sometime shortly after all this started, my dad told me that he was leaving her. I thought to myself, *Good! Everyone wants to leave! Me too!*

You must also remember that, deep in my heart, I was always a daddy's girl. In my heart, I sided with him, while wrestling with my mother's broken heart. I was deeply torn. It was too much for me, and in my own way, I ran too. I asked if I could go up to Minnesota and live with my great aunt and uncle. Much to my surprise, everyone agreed that I could go.

That summer before I left, I spent my fifteenth birthday all alone. Dad had moved out with his girlfriend, and Mom took my sister up north to Minnesota—neither remembered my birthday that year. They had other things on their minds. I spent that night home alone, wandering around in the dark—crying. There was a deep sense of loneliness growing inside me. My happy little world was shaken, and I had no idea what to do and had no one to talk to.

It was my first Greyhound bus trip that August. I pretended that I was going to college. The bus broke down that night between Chicago and Duluth and set us behind schedule several hours, so I missed my transfer to Grand Rapids. I sat at the bus depot for several hours before I got the courage to call my uncle and tell him what happened. There were no cell phones back then, and I seriously did not deal with that problem well.

Romans 6:23 reads, "For the wages of sin is death, but the free gift of God is eternal life" (ESV).

Our family had sinned against God, and there was this shadow of death hovering over us—eagerly waiting to make that death permanent. I did not know it then, but we had a redeemer watching carefully over us all. He was waiting until we had come to the end of ourselves. It is a good thing to come to the end of ourselves, though some take longer than others. But God watches and quietly waits—patiently—for those who belong to him. He alone is the true and loving Father we all long for.

Chapter 6

This morning as I woke up, there was an old song running through my heart. I was singing it to myself. I can't say that it is one that I think of frequently, maybe not for decades, but as I am sorting through old memories and continuing my journey here, it seems to belong.

"I sing because I'm happy. I sing because I am free, for his eye is on the sparrow, and I know He's watching me."

He was and is watching me—I just didn't know it at this point.

On we go—

The weight of the sin in my family was heavy like a thick blanket, and it seemed to blot out all light for me. I couldn't see anything, but I pressed on with feelings of deep aloneness. I stumbled around in the dark.

I actually wasn't alone, but that was hard to see at fifteen, and feelings felt like everything to me. This was the place in the road when some very significant people joined me in my journey. At that age, it is hard to recognize who is there for the long run and who will disappear like a vapor. I didn't know, even though that is the age that you *do* think you know everything. I thought I did, but I didn't. I smile as the jingle runs through my mind: "Make new friends but keep the old—one is silver and the other gold."

These are gold—my longest friend lived across the street from me as a child. Her name is Linda, as well. I lost track of her for many, many years. We had searched for each other, but as girls change their names when they marry, it was nearly impossible. It took a long time to find each other, but it was always meant to be. We both live in

Minnesota now, even though we met in Illinois. God is whispering to her as well and calling her name. How marvelous God is!

As for me, it is a comforting piece of my puzzle—seeing again that God lined up my friends even back then. My next forever friend is Mary, a good Catholic girl. Our hearts bonded in tenth grade back in Grand Rapids when I lived with my great uncle Charlie and aunt Eunice. We had many discussions about God, as our Catholic and Baptist beliefs were miles apart. But we clung to each other with great, forever love.

It was another God thing. We both had three sons and one daughter, and God was calling both of our names. I am continuously amazed and grateful as I have followed his footprints all along my pathway during those dark and fearful years.

And from these years, last but not least is Kathy. She was the youngest child of Charlie and Eunice. She became my second sister and has been my forever friend. There has never been sibling rivalry, for which I am grateful. She, too, has heard God whispering her name.

The prophet Jeremiah speaks God's heart when he writes. Jeremiah 31:3 (KJV) reads, "I have loved thee with an everlasting love and with loving kindness I have drawn thee."

When I was younger, I was so confused about what love really is. Honestly, I was confused about this for most of my life.

People who are supposed to love you don't seem to. You wonder if it is your fault, like maybe you are doing something wrong, maybe you are not good enough, maybe you are not pretty enough. I even thought that God loved me a little less because of the family he gave to me. I believed lies for a long time.

Many people certainly want you to believe that problems are your fault—if only you would do such and such better. I believed that. So I spent many years trying to do what I thought other people wanted me to do. I spent most of the years of my life (in my own way) begging those around me to love me. It never seemed to work.

I took the blame onto myself and, as a result, struggled with self-worth for a long time.

I will tell you, at this point, that my great uncle Charlie was my first real love. He loved me like a true father would. He never wavered for forty years. He never looked at my failures, and I saw joy in his eyes every time I visited. I just loved him. I just loved him. I just loved him. I can't say it enough. Unlike my earthly father, he saw value in me and treated me as someone to cherish, not because I did something for him but just because I was me. He was a gift to me.

For the two years before he passed away, I cried and cried because I knew that he would soon be gone and I didn't want to lose my replacement father.

The day we had his funeral, my grandson Owen was born. I see that God. Thank you. But that was forty years later, and I was still fifteen, and my family was broken. It would be a long time until I found that happy little girl again. At that time, I had forgotten who she was. I had forgotten that quiet whisper calling my name.

Chapter 7

Isaiah 49:16 (HCSB) reads, "Look, I have inscribed you on the palms of My hands."

There it was—my name written clearly and boldly on his notebook. Linda—

I had my first boyfriend in ninth grade. He was tall, dark, and very handsome. He was also a Mexican, and in those days, white girls only dated white boys. Society didn't look kindly upon those kinds of things, and I watched as the race riots of the sixties exploded into violence. Nonetheless, he was my boyfriend, and we spent considerable time together, even though in reality, it wasn't long—but it was long enough for me to try and learn Spanish.

He was a year older than I was, and he came from a large family on the poor side of town. He had a car that we would scoop the loop in. That meant driving up and down Grand Avenue, downtown Waukegan, Illinois, along with many other teenage couples—back and forth. It was a form of dating in those days.

One day, he talked me into skipping school. I missed the morning classes, but I was fearful and went back that afternoon. I was called to the office where I begged the counselor to let me tell my mother. She agreed. My boyfriend found a woman who called and pretended that she was my mother. I never once skipped school again. I believed that I was in love.

Charlie and I would later argue about that for some time. He was right.

Not long after that, my boyfriend decided to quit school and join the Army. The Vietnam War was going full boar, and immediately after basic, he was deployed. I was there the day he got on the bus.

Shortly after he arrived in Vietnam, he sent me an engagement ring and asked me to wait for him. I agreed, but sometime later, I received a letter that clearly showed that he was taking some kind of drugs. Looking back, I understand now—but I was deathly afraid of anything to do with drugs or alcohol, and I ended the relationship. Later, he would come back looking for me, but it was too late.

I think about him sometimes with fond memories.

But there it was—my name written on his notebook, and it was a week before the turn-around dance. That meant that the girls were supposed to ask the boys to the dance. I asked him, and he agreed. So Fred and I became a couple for a very short time.

I can't say what he was thinking or his memories of those early days, but he seemed to seriously pursue me. It felt nice, but our first date after the dance was his promise to take me out to his sister's place where they had horses. Now I have to say here that I just loved horses. Horse books were my favorite kind to read. I would read them over and over. My cousins in Illinois had horses, and I was seriously envious of them.

Horses were strong and beautiful, and somehow, my romantic dreams were of some prince charming, riding on a horse and sweeping me away to live happily ever after.

These things filled much of my thoughts. But that was not what happened.

We drove out to their home and wandered over to where the horses were and just stood there. He had promised we could ride them. I waited and waited and waited in silence. We left in continued silence. I was not happy, and on the way home, he admitted that he had never even asked if we could ride. I told him to stop the car.

He did. I got out. I walked back to the far side of a small bridge behind us and stood on the other side. He waited but never got out to look for me. Then he drove away, leaving me to walk back to my uncle's. That ended that.

Tenth grade ended, and I went back home to Illinois and my mother's tears. I would have much preferred to stay at my aunt and uncle's, but my call of duty was with my mom.

As I started eleventh grade, I learned that my cousin had told everyone that I had gone away the year before because I was pregnant. Really? There was no safe person in my life down there. So as a result, I had no friends the rest of high school. The only exceptions to that were two nice Christian girls who befriended me and sat with me at lunch. They invited me to their homes and tried very hard to get me to become a Christian. I thought that I was a Christian, but apparently, they knew better. I was broken inside—sad and lonely. Both of my parents had emotionally abandoned me. My siblings were gone. I continued to go to school and began working, as I was on my own as far as money was concerned after the age of fourteen.

I was alone, and my mother was crying.

That year passed slowly, and with eagerness, I planned a trip back up to Minnesota to visit my aunt and uncle. While there, somehow, Fred and I talked, and I was amazed that, after a year, he still liked me. I was impressed with his faithfulness and thought that was an admirable quality. I decided to give him another chance. Deep inside, I had come to the conclusion that if I wanted to escape my mother's tears, I needed to get married. I thought about going to college, but without any support from my parents, that felt hopeless.

I was so broken inside that I doubted that anyone else would ever ask me to marry. Deep inside, I was in love with being in love. Deep inside, I believed all the fairy-tale fantasies of living happily ever after. Surely, not everyone was like my parents, and I thought I would be different.

Christmas of my senior year—Fred asked me to marry him, and he gave me a beautiful ring. I said yes, and we planned an August wedding. I would be eighteen, and he would be nineteen.

We were both extreme introverts and continued in our own unspoken worlds and dreams, unaware that dreams are just that—and are easily shattered. We were both kind people, quiet, and children who had not yet grown up. We meant well enough.

As I finished up my senior year in high school, I wore my engagement ring proudly. I was now someone who had someone who wanted to be with me. I had value.

I was engaged. There was no help from either of my parents with the plans for our wedding. There was no help from Fred either. I was on my own, but I was lost in my own dreamworld and made my plans. I sewed my own dress, sent out invitations, ordered flowers, ordered a cake, arranged for food and decorations, and even got a kind man from church to take our pictures. I asked my dad if he would help me with some of the bills. He agreed to give me $100.

In the end, he refused to give me any money, until I showed him all the receipts of the bills already paid for. I was deeply, deeply hurt and offended.

I graduated from high school with neither of my parents attending the ceremony. I pressed forward with my life, without the support of my father or mother or sister or brother or an awareness of God.

I had expectations that my new husband would be my best friend—lover—and that our children would be conceived in passionate joy and deep intimate love forever. Such is the introvert world of a romantic eighteen-year-old girl—at least me.

That did not turn out to be what happened.

I was the first of us three kids to marry, and I became Linda Jean Schmidt on August 16, 1969. Some of Fred's family came down from Minnesota (I liked them). Charlie and Eunice came as well. But there was a big fight going on because my mom refused to let my dad bring his new wife to the wedding, and in all fairness to my mom, my parents had just gotten divorced. My mother had refused to divorce him until he threatened to call us kids into court, so my dad walked me down the aisle but was not too happy about it. That issue became a continued one as my brother and sister married in the future.

After the ceremony, we drove to Toronto, Canada, for our honeymoon. I did not like Detroit, Michigan, and have never been there since. As all the plans for the wedding and honeymoon had been totally left to me, I had forgotten to plan for our first night, as it was a two-day drive to Toronto.

I was excited about our first adventure, but as the day went on, Fred refused to stop until it got very late, and by the time he did, we found ourselves in a very small town with no motel. That first night, we slept in a gravel pit—in very hot weather so the windows were rolled down.

In the morning, I was covered with bug bites. They were probably mosquito bites, but I had so many that I had an allergic reaction and ended up at a doctor's office in Toronto. When we got to our hotel reservation, I thought he would sign us in as Mr. and Mrs. Fred Schmidt, which was not what he did. He just signed Fred Schmidt and left me standing there with the clerk looking at me.

We were both so young, and I was deeply embarrassed and very touchy about those things. To say the least, I was easily offended. My prince charming shouldn't forget that I was now his wife two days after we had married.

As our honeymoon progressed, our car engine caught on fire, and there was a large unexpected repair bill, along with several other problems we encountered. They seem rather trite now, but they seemed very large to me back then—and by the time our two-week honeymoon was over, I was not a happy camper.

I was trying to avoid problems, but they seemed to appear everywhere, and I was married to a man who refused to talk. He said that I married him this way and that he didn't have to change. For me, things never improved from that point.

I had never learned how to cook or clean, nor did he, so our first apartment, which was in a private home on the second floor, became so filthy that we were actually asked to leave after the first year.

He would later tell me, jokingly of course (and I never joked), that his definition of a wife was "someone you screw on a bed, and she cooked and cleaned for you." He would not help cook or clean. Period. The pressure increased in my heart, along with the devastating discovery of an addiction to pornography, which many years in the future, along with his refusal to talk to me, would lead to divorce.

But back then, I began to weep from loneliness. Why did I think that someone who rarely talked before marriage would after marriage? I did—as I began to grow up. He did not. He was the baby of thirteen, and that was how he viewed himself—the baby with no desire to grow up. So I became his mother and my mother's mother.

Ugh! But I had no choice—so I cried and cried. Marriage did not take away my loneliness—it only made it worse. It shattered my very deep dreams.

Fairy tales had tricked me. The deep need to be loved was not found in marriage, and now, I was locked into a legally committed marriage for the rest of my life with someone who refused to talk to me. I just cried. Divorce was a sin.

But that is for another time, and I need to say, at this point, that with all of the struggles with our marriage and failures to find peace with each other, I have few regrets. My recompense is four marvelous children and, at this time, eight beautiful grandchildren.

But my very best gift from all of this is that I found the love I was really looking for—and that would be Jesus. Fred and I have deeply forgiven each other long ago and remain forever friends. It is always easier to see things looking back than it is walking through the darkness.

So two years into the marriage, I longed for a baby. I only wanted to have daughters, as I was genuinely afraid of having sons. I was afraid of them having to go to war. I was afraid that they would turn out like all the other men I knew and didn't like.

But as always, God knew what I really needed, so then in his kindness to me, he gave me a daughter.

Chapter 8

John 3:3 (ESV) reads, "Unless one is born again, he cannot see the kingdom of God."

The English dictionary gives several antonyms for the word *see*: "disbelieve, disregard, miss, ignore, look away, overlook."

Jesus defined it more clearly. He just simply stated that if you don't see, you are blind.

It was early in the afternoon that she was born. Our daughter, Michelle Christine Schmidt, arrived on June 9, 1972—three weeks before her due date. I had played volleyball two days earlier, which brought on her arrival. I had been determined to use the Lamaze Method, which used breathing techniques and no pain meds. I did, and though it might seem strange, I loved the process of giving birth and always did. There was an excitement I had never experienced before. It was something powerful, the unknown, something bigger than me—like Christmas morning but a hundred times more filled with excitement and expectations. I loved it and still cherish those moments.

I was so happy that I had a little daughter to love. She was a gift to me. I knew it was a miracle.

And then the moment came—fear swept over me like a flood. She cried and cried and cried, and I had no idea what to do. I had never been around infants. I held her and rocked her and fed her and changed her, and she cried. Please stop crying. Please! Fred was no help. He hadn't even washed the dishes while I was in the hospital for three days. My mother had to come and do that. I was trying to heal from giving birth and nursing a baby. I became filled with fear that I would fail at being a mother. I had no older women in my life close to me. My mother was still crying and overwhelmed by her own problems. I was pushed into a corner with nowhere to go—desperate. I didn't know that God was using this little girl to help me find something that I needed.

So I prayed and cried out to God—

Somewhere in there, I had a thought, or God spoke to me—I don't know which. I thought that God said to me, "I am a good Father. Maybe you should get to know me, and I can teach you how to love your children."

It was a thought anyway. I had no idea how I would get to know him. isn't knowing God what I had—and just being good? I was trying to do that, but I was desperate, and I didn't want to fail my beloved daughter. She was someone more important than I was—she was a reason beyond myself to search for answers.

Except one be born again—what is that? In John chapter 3, the religious man, a teacher of the Jewish people, Nicodemus, asked the same question. I had just experienced giving birth to a little girl. She was born—born again? Born a second time?

I remembered my second-grade teacher. Our church had always talked about having a personal relationship with Jesus. I had prayed that prayer several times. I couldn't see. I was in the dark. I couldn't see or understand, but I knew I was desperate. So I prayed.

Two very strange things happened shortly after Michelle was born. Both happened in the morning—

There was a knock at my door. It was my sister, Wendy. This was very unusual as our relationship was very distant at best. She was sobbing and asked to come in. What I remember is, that morning, God had spoken clearly to her that she had to choose—choose to stay with the married man she was living with *or* choose God. She was very scared, and in my opinion, it took a lot to get her scared. I mean, she had gotten into fights with Black girls in high school and had gotten beaten up. She was tough—whoa, God had scared my sister? He had talked to her? God had scared my sister enough to make her move out? So she moved in with us for a few days. I remember that she had an eye infection from her contacts while she was there. I was shaken. God frightened my sister enough to make her do something? Whoa!

A month later, the second big thing happened. Paul and Mary were a couple at our Baptist church, both of whom I couldn't ignore. I was jealous of them. Paul loved Mary. She had something that I didn't have. Her husband loved her. I could see it. I watched them all the time. He was the youth leader for the teens; he attended Trinity Seminary in Chicago, working on becoming a pastor; he worked full-time; they had two little daughters; he loved his wife.

One morning on the way to work, a guy was running from the police down Lewis Avenue, and his car hit Paul's car and killed Paul instantly. There were tracts about Jesus all over the road. I went into shock—didn't the Bible promise that if you honored your father and mother, you would live a long life? Paul should have lived a very long life. He was dead. I didn't understand.

At the funeral, Mary was covered in black—even over her face. I cried and cried and cried—for her, for me, for everything I could think of.

I will never forget the Sunday morning one month later. I sat alone in the very back pew at church and watched in disbelief as Mary got up to sing. I was horrified! How could she sing after her beloved husband had just died? Then it happened—I heard a voice inside my heart simply and clearly say, "She has something you don't have." It was what that voice said, but more than that, it was the gentleness and love that I had never heard before—something my heart craved to hear again.

I went home that morning and did the only thing I knew to do—I started to read my Bible and pray. The words just seemed like empty words, but I hungered to hear that voice again. I needed to. I had to find it. I waited and listened, but nothing happened. I quit, as I do easily. Then I remembered that voice and started the process again. Nothing seemed to happen again. I did this repeatedly for ten months.

May came around, and our church was sending a bus to Chicago for a seminar called "Basic Youth Conflicts." It was for three evenings and all day of Saturday. I signed Fred and myself up for it. I had never left Michelle before and had to leave her at my mom's. She cried most of the time.

It was a ten-mile drive from our home to my mom's and then to the church to catch the bus. I will never forget that, on those drives every day, we never hit one red light, and there where at least a dozen. God turned those lights green for me, which was a very small miracle. But I noticed, and I remember.

Something happened greater than that miracle the first night—God opened up my eyes, and I could see I had been blind and in darkness, and for the first time in my life, I saw that I was loved. I cried deeply as he flooded my heart with himself, his forgiveness, and I experienced being born again. He had heard my cries and had rescued me. God is much more than words, more than believing religious things, more than being good, more than I ever imagined. His love is very real. It overwhelmed me—

I was once in darkness Now my eyes can see I was lost until Jesus sought and found me. Oh, what love he offers. Oh, what peace he gives. I will sing forevermore he lives.

Chapter 9

Jeremiah 29:13–14a (NASB) reads, "'And you will seek Me and find Me when you search for me with all your heart. I will let Myself be found by you,' declares the Lord."

I don't think that I came down from cloud 9 for several months. The Bible that used to be so hard and meaningless to me became alive with love and meaning and flooded my heart with joy and hope and purpose, as though it had been written directly to me.

Unless a man be born again, he cannot see the kingdom of God. I got it. I was like a brand-new baby, loved and totally enjoying life, as I shifted from the darkness of sin into the light—the weight of my sin had been removed and forgiven by the sacrifice Jesus paid on the cross to make me his own. He saved me. I was lost—now, I was rescued. I couldn't believe that I had not heard or understood this before. But I spent hours every day in God's Word, memorizing it and talking to God. He was my new friend. I was deeply grateful, and I could never thank him enough.

Two weeks after this all happened, Fred and I moved our mobile home up to Minnesota. Everything was new. I can't remember why, but it was a good move. I was puzzled though—Fred had not heard God at those seminars. How could he not have? God couldn't have been clearer to me. Why had he not talked to Fred? He had no idea what had happened to me. I tried to tell him. He didn't understand. All I knew was that I was happy. I searched for a church to go to, believing that the Baptist church was the only church that taught the truth. The only one around was in Mound, Minnesota, so we went. I was disappointed that morning when there didn't seem to be anyone there who was excited about God. That's not to say that there wasn't anyone like that. How would I have really known? That was fifty years ago, and there is no longer a Baptist church in Mound. I was looking for someone excited about God to talk to.

That next week, I ran into a young man, who was driving a bus every Sunday picking up kids to go to church in Maple Plain. He was excited about God. We tried his church. The pastor was Burnie Drew, and he was excited about God. But what was really important was, as I sat in the adult Sunday school class that week, a woman named Mary Printy was teaching, and she was saying the exact things God was saying to me that week. Someone else was hearing what I was hearing from God. She had my attention. I became devoted to her for many years. She taught me many scripture songs and brought me to many Spirit-filled meetings. I couldn't learn enough. The deepest desire of my heart was to learn to know God's voice and to learn his ways. He heard my prayers and set me on a course to learn just that. I just didn't like the lessons that I had to learn. They were not what I expected. To this day, I am forever grateful and wouldn't trade what I learned for anything this world has to offer. Needless to say, I didn't learn willingly. I somehow thought that knowing God meant I would be rescued from all my troubles. That is not true in many respects. And I didn't like it one bit.

Psalm 127:1 reads, "Unless the Lord builds the house, the builders labor in vain" (NIV).

Before I go forward with my story, it is necessary to go back. A life, a marriage, a family will only be as good as the foundation upon which it is built. Whether it is visible for all to see is irrelevant, the storms of life expose what it has been built on and will either cause it to stand or fall—or reveal one's willingness to live in wreckage.

Some do—I couldn't.

Jesus told a story in the gospel of Matthew about two men. One man built his house on a rock, while the other built his house on the sand. Upon both houses, the rain fell, and the river rose—the winds blew and pounded down on them. One house stood firm, while the other fell and collapsed.

What you build your life on, your marriage on, your family on matters—and I learned that if the builders are both broken or if only one is willing to work on it, it is tough to build anything of quality. The good news is that in the storms of life, Jesus is always waiting to throw you a lifeline. There is always hope, but one must grab onto the rope that God offers. The other good news is that everyone walks through the storms (I didn't know this)—everyone walks through them because everyone needs a lifeline. What will you hold onto?

Many times, we grab onto things made of sand, and our lives become shattered. Sand is never a good material to build a solid foundation upon. Jesus called the two men in his parable—the wise man and the foolish man. Only one of their houses withstood the storm. It is always wise to follow an expert's instructions. Jesus is the master builder.

Looking back on those years is somewhat a blur to me. It was a long time ago—and as I have previously stated, Fred and I have long since forgiven each other and remained friends. We were both so young, so broken, ill-equipped, naive, and certainly not working together as a team. It was hard to build well in those circumstances. We meant well, but meaning well has little to do with building well—

Fred was always a hard worker. In the early years, the direction of what he should do for a living was unclear, but he always worked—first for Allen his brother-in-law, then the Delano Granite Works, then a paper company in Long Lake, to finally choosing sheet rocking, starting with his brother Merle. He was a faithful and hard worker. I will forever be grateful that after the children came, I was able to stay home with them. I just loved being a mother.

Fred never seemed angry, nor did he ever intentionally say mean or hurtful things to me. He was easygoing despite his continual silence.

Although we never spoke about it—I assumed, like me, that he feared conflict.

I feared conflict for two reasons—both were rooted in my insecurities.

I was afraid of conflict because I had no experience in solving problems. I was not an angry person nor a rude person—yelling or nagging were not part of who I was.

The second reason was my fear that a problem would expose and destroy the relationship. I was not sure that I was loved enough to survive an unsolved problem. I was unsure that I was loved. This fear haunted me.

Fred told me, "I told you once that I loved you, and if that changes, I will let you know." For someone who never talked to me, that was not a wise thing to say, especially since I had no sense of humor. Again, I lived in continuous fear.

I believed a lie (many insecure people do). I believed that confronting a problem would always end in a permanently broken relationship, which I never wanted. But that was what I interpreted from my parents and, to be quite honest, over the years from all of my family of origin except my mother.

Self-centered love lasts only for a period. Problems were a test of love's genuineness—and I preferred to not know the truth. Truth sometimes breaks our hearts.

In looking back at it, I needed someone to love me more than I knew how to love.

Needing is not the same as loving.

Anyways, we had some good foundations—hardworking, peaceable, and though we were poor, we had good financial habits. We never wasted money on things we didn't have money for. We had my savings from high school, which we used to buy a mobile home and later to buy our home in Maple Plain on Bryant Street.

By the time Michelle was born, we were debt-free, thus enabling me to be a stay-at-home mother, though I later earned babysitting money to help out. I sacrificed everything I needed and bought things at garage sales for many years. Within seven years, our home was paid for, which gave us some wiggle room. We went without a refrigerator for a time, and one year, there was no money for house insurance.

The kids didn't have a lot, but they had what they needed.

One more thing that I will always appreciate was that Fred let me tithe after I became a Christian. I learned that everything we had was from God, and he was a giver. I tried to show him my gratitude. Early on in our tithing, we were audited once.

You can never outgive God. So there was some good foundation stones there, but the ones we were missing were the ones that did great damage to Fred and me and our children. I wish today that I could say that I was grown up enough to make it through them, but I wasn't. The ones that destroyed our foundation were immaturity, selfishness, dishonesty, and a refusal to communicate and work through problems.

In the end, we had sixteen years of undealt-with issues that had become an enormous mountain. In the end, it was a mountain I had given up on and was unwilling to climb.

And Fred, well, you would have to ask him. We both have regrets—

Chapter 10

James 1:17 (ESV) reads, "Every good gift and every perfect gift is from above, coming down from the Father."

I am a very fortunate and blessed person. I am well aware of that. With all my heart, I am grateful.

Though receiving gifts is not my love language, through the years, I have come to understand that a good gift is that which comes from someone, not only from one who loves you, but it is something uniquely special to you, something very personal (I am not speaking of intimacy), and something that lasts. God gives good gifts.

In contrast, it is not like a toy one gives their child at Christmas and it is played with for a week and broken. I am not saying that one should not give such gifts. I am saying that a good gift will be something that you recognize and cherish, and it does something deep inside your heart. It is not something you forget.

That is not to say that you can't give someone something very special and the person you give it to does not recognize it for what it is. That happens all the time. They may be blind to it because of the condition of their hearts.

I have learned that many people's hearts are hardened and can't see value in much of anything. Or people have more than they need and take things for granted.

You have to be looking, and as we have talked about blindness in the previous chapter, it is sometimes something hard to see.

Many good gifts are not material. When you are young and come from a poorer upbringing, material things seem to have great value. In the end, the joy doesn't last long. Material wealth can trick you, and you find that you need more and more for happiness—but that is a vain thing as well. In the end, your hands will still be empty and your heart will too. Good gifts received will be accompanied with gratitude.

Genuine thankfulness is its companion. You will not forget them.

As I write this, and it is the week of Thanksgiving, may this book be a written record of my gratitude and thankfulness for the innumerable good gifts I have received.

I have received many. I see some of them clearly. Anything that comes from a heart of love to another is a good gift. Many good gifts come with some kind of a cost—many cost great sacrifice.

On the very top of the list of tangible good gifts I have received in this life will always be my children and, now, my grandchildren. They are special beyond words to me—each one is a treasure no amount of wealth could ever buy. They are good gifts from my Father.

I just was filled with so much love for my daughter as she came into our world. I worried about what I would do when my other children came. Could I love them as much?

She was so smart. She amazed me with her memory. I love being her mother. I couldn't say that too much. I love being a mother. I threw my heart into it all. It filled up the void that was missing from my marriage and distracted me for many years. The loves of my life became—God and my children.

Deep inside, my heart longed for Fred to be my friend, but he wasn't talking, and I didn't have time to remain in an adolescent state. I had a child to love and care for. I grew up from that point in life. Immaturity was not a luxury I had to choose from. The responsibilities of life were not an option, and I took them on seriously and completely. One of my faults has always been that I was so serious.

Fred worked, and I pretty much did everything else. Three months after I was born again, I became pregnant with Michael. I knew the next morning, for whatever reason, and I was so excited! I was ready for a son, and God gave me my heart's desire.

Fred never seemed to have any input as to names, so Michael Frederick Schmidt it was. He was born on May 15, 1974, on his due date.

I loved the whole state of pregnancy and delivery, and my heart expanded again with an explosion of love. I just loved him too!

I just loved this mother thing! Taking care of two children twenty-three months apart was a lot of work, but I never—ever—for one moment regretted it.

It was at this time that my mother wasn't happy, being away from me down in Illinois. My brother went and packed her up and moved her. She sold the house she had received in the divorce and came to Minnesota—bought a mobile home and put it in the trailer park, a block from where we lived. Alan packed her up, put her next to me, and left to go back to his family. That was where she always wanted to be—next to me. As the oldest daughter or because of my temperament, whatever, it became my job for the rest of her life—for me to take care of my mom.

My brother and sister would come up to visit once in a while, but he lived farther away. Wendy came more often—twice a year (I think). Mom living a block away from me was too close, and a month after she moved to Minnesota, we sold our trailer and bought the house in Maple Plain on Bryant Street. We lived there for thirteen years.

I was ten miles from my mother, and that was a good distance. She had finally learned to drive and came over often, but she was still crying and crying.

I remember that first fall on Bryant Street. I was burning some leaves in the driveway, and from somewhere unknown to me, the smoke gave me poison sumac all over my face and arms. I was horrified. I was nursing a young baby, and my mother had to come and stay because I needed someone to hold him while he nursed. I was terrified of spreading the poison onto Michael. I thought that my face would be forever scarred and ugly beyond words—this might be a good time to tell you that, for many years, I truly thought that I was ugly.

I hated my name because its meaning is pretty. I thought it was a cruel joke that I had been given such an ill-fitted name. Those were the years that I still believed that men only loved beautiful women. That was why I was unloved. I would have denied it at that time, but I believed it deep in my heart. That was true. It is the message that the world declares loudly all the time. If you hear it enough times, it becomes true to you. I believed that, since I would never be pretty, I had to be very nice to be loved, but that didn't work either.

So when I got poison sumac, it was disastrous to me.

Sometime later, God would give to me a scripture verse, and I stopped hating my name.

Names are important. It was from Isaiah 61:3 (KJV):

> To appoint unto them that mourn in Zion, to give unto them beauty for ashes, the oil of joy for mourning, the garment of praise for the spirit of heaviness; that they might be called trees of righteousness, the planting of the Lord, that He might be glorified.

I then understood and no longer hated my name.

God was going to take the ashes of my life—and there were plenty—and turn them into something beautiful. He knew what he was doing back on July 16, 1951. I was at peace. He didn't make a mistake.

This was also the time in my life that I had to face the tremendous fear I had of the dark. I would lie awake at night in the dark and stare at the doorway for fear that something was going to come into the room. I was also fearful of going outside in the dark at night.

There is no doubt that these things overwhelmed me because of the past episodes in my youth with my brother, but I also found that, as I had become alive to God as a Christian—and God was unseen yet so real—the spiritual world of evil was also something very real. I had to battle to not let it overwhelm me.

I spent a month, every night, saying a scripture verse from Psalm 139 over and over.

It was verse 12: "Even darkness is not dark to You. And the night is as bright as the day; darkness and light are alike to You" (NASB). With God's help, I faced this fear, and much to my amazement, I have never feared the darkness again in my life. It a was victory!

After Michael was born, I thought that I made a deal with God that I would trust him with the issue of birth control. I knew that I wanted four children but was not yet ready to take on my third child. I went merrily on my way until I realized that I was two and a half months pregnant. I was mad at God. He hadn't warned me.

I didn't talk to him for a month.

But after that period, I missed talking to the one who loved me, and I was sorry. God knew what he was doing. He always does. He was sending me a gift. It would be my beloved son Matthew. The name Matthew means "a gift from God." It also means "recompense." The name David means "beloved."

I was three and a half months pregnant when Fred told me he didn't love me anymore and that he loved someone else. That night, I went to a church meeting in the cities, and to be honest, I don't know what happened, but for the first time in my life, I had a block in my brain (out of shock? I don't know)—all I know is that it didn't register. I went on with my pregnancy, in love with this new baby coming.

He, too, came on his due date. Matthew David Schmidt. September 18, 1976. My mom had tried to tell me but couldn't. Fred brought her up to the hospital to see the baby. She was just a teenager from our church and a sweet girl.

Later, I would counsel with her and asked her not to even speak to him, as even speaking to him was encouraging him. She hadn't meant for this to happen and willingly did as I asked—as far as I knew. It became time for me to leave this church I loved. To put it mildly, I was in shock as I faced the brokenness of our marriage. I had three small children and no income. I had little choice.

I was almost in the same place my mother had found herself in. How did that happen?

I will admit that, from that point on, I hated being married to him. But the real truth was I hated being married to someone who didn't love me. Somewhere in my heart, I knew that I was created to be loved. Why wasn't I?

Feeling that way was not what the Bible taught, and I struggled from that point on.

I was deeply touched as God showed me the meaning of the name Matthew. Matthew's name not only meant a gift from God but also a recompense. God gave him to me to make up for the hurt in my heart. He was my recompense. He represented God's tender, compassionate love for me expressed in something tangible, and that is what Matthew always was from the beginning—a sweet loving little boy. I called him honey boy. Fred would call him honey toad. I did my best to forgive, but that didn't even remotely heal the deep pain of betrayal in my heart.

I also watched as Matthew deeply loved his father, and in that, I saw God's great mercy.

I started attending the Mound Assembly of God church. Life changed.

I nursed Matthew for two years and became pregnant for the fourth time immediately after I stopped. In the third month of that pregnancy, I miscarried.

I remember it clearly. It was the time that I started going to a brand-new church called El Shaddai. That would be where I met my lifelong girlfriend, Barb Barnes. The doctor had told me not to get pregnant for six months, but as I got pregnant easily, I was pregnant again six weeks later.

My youngest and greatly loved son Mark John Schmidt was on his way. He was born two days after his due date on October 2, 1979. I was ecstatic. I didn't have time to mourn the loss of the little daughter I had miscarried. God was so good to me. He told me all the time how much he loved me, but I would go home to my husband, who didn't, and it was hard to reconcile. I wrestled with the belief that if God loved me—wouldn't he have my husband love me too? It was so hard. I filled the void with just loving my children.

Psalm 103 has some of my favorite verses:

> For as high as the heavens are above the earth, so great is His steadfast love towards those who fear Him. As far as the east is from the west, so far does He remove our transgressions from us. As a father shows compassion to his children, so the Lord shows compassion on those who fear Him. For He knows our frame; he remembers that we are dust—
>
> But the steadfast love of the Lord is from everlasting to everlasting on those who fear Him, and His righteousness to children's children to those who keep His covenant, who remember to do His commandments. (ESV)

It is a promise I believe for my children and grandchildren. I have certainly failed in many ways, but I have learned that his mercy triumphs over judgment.

Chapter 11

Genesis 2:18 reads, "Then the Lord God said, 'It is not good that the man should be alone; I will make him a helper fit for him'" (ESV).

I have always asked many questions, which has bothered some people in my life. I never meant for it to bother them. I want to know things and am always searching; my brain is always processing, and it is never quiet.

That puts an introvert into a strange place. We may not be talking, but we are thinking.

I love to talk to others and enjoy a good conversation. I am just poor at recognizing who wants to talk and poor at starting conversations. There have been long periods in my life where I have struggled with condemnation for my poor ability to converse with other people.

My best friend Barb is so good at talking to people, and I watched her one time go around a room, having conversations with each person and making them smile. I envied her. I just wanted to be like her, until I realized we are all different and I was who I was created to be—so was she. It was *okay*.

I remember trying so very hard to teach Michael, when he was young, how to talk about things that were bothering him. It was a game called twenty questions.

Sometimes, we don't talk because there are difficult things to say. Other people just refuse to talk—I know a few. Communication is a basic human need. Many problems are created when we don't. Communicating from our hearts can take work and looking honestly at our own selves. It is easy to blame others. It is easy to believe a lie.

As I grew up in my twenties, I adopted my own definition of the word *love*: "If you love me, talk to me." I then adopted the belief: "If you don't talk to me, you don't love me." It can be a dangerous place living in your own little world. That is why writing is necessary for me. People only listen if they want to.

So my question is—why do people marry? What is their real reason?

I am sure that there are many different reasons, but why do they really?

I believe God with all my heart when he says that it is not good to be alone. We were made for relationship. It is in our DNA.

I know that there are vast numbers of people who live alone, either by choice, by divorce, by death, or they simply never find someone who truly loves them. Maybe some are afraid to even look. It is hard to love someone when you don't love yourself. It is hard to love when you do not know God. He is the source of true love.

Some people truly want to live their life unmarried. The apostle Paul was single, John the Baptist was single. I know a few women who chose to never married and felt called to live that way. It can be a touchy subject, but that is not the purpose of my inquiry.

My question is, what is the underlying reason people choose to marry? Is it their need to be loved and connected? Do they want to have children and a family? Is it for sex or because a child is coming? Do people marry to not sin against God's commandments? Do they marry for money or material possessions? Is a woman looking for someone to protect her, provide for her, give her value? Does a man marry because a woman is beautiful and nice to look at? Do aggressive people look for someone easy to dominate? Or do compliant people look for others to make decisions for them?

Many times, people choose someone the opposite of them. What percentage of people marry because they genuinely care about the welfare of the person they have committed their lives to? I don't know.

Statistics show that we as humans struggle with these issues. I have struggled, and let's get this elephant in the room out in the open—I have failed.

Fred was the thirteenth child of Fred and Edna Schmidt. He had nine sisters and three brothers. One sister passed away before I met him, so he had eight sisters. He was the baby.

I was told he didn't walk until he was two because his sisters would carry him all the time. His mother passed away sometime around the age of twelve, so he was without a mother. His father loved to argue and was hard on him—making him work hard on the farm.

Though Fred was easygoing, he had anger issues with his father (the only person I ever knew Fred was angry with.) Fred was not an angry person in general. There were things he needed to forgive, and I attest to the fact that forgiving one's parents is not an easy or quickly done task. It takes a deep heart-searching and time.

I liked his father and think that he liked me a little. He would chew tobacco and spit in a coffee can by his chair. That was a little gross, but I never had to clean it, so it was not an issue with me. His older brother Arnold was injured badly in the Vietnam war and was living disabled on the farm with their father. That was sad. But he was strong—at least that was what I saw. Fred's dad and Arnold argued a lot.

I remember the old farmhouse. We slept upstairs where there were holes in the walls and you could hear the bats up in the attic. I always liked Fred's family, and though his sisters didn't like the other two sisters-in-law, I always felt accepted.

As sisters, they got along well, and I liked that. They drank coffee all of the time. I hated coffee. (I drink it now but need coffee creamer). I would never drink it black.

The other thing that they would do is play cards. They asked me several times if I wanted to learn how to play, but I didn't. They would stay up until all hours of the night, playing cards, and maybe, they still do. That was hard because I was never a late-night person. I have always been a morning person, and I always had young children to care for and was a light sleeper.

I was tired. I tried staying up late, but it never worked for me. I was fond of them, especially Denise, Fred's niece. We have always had a special bond all these years. I love her.

In late Summer of 1978, when Matthew was almost two, Fred's dad was diagnosed with cancer and passed away very quickly. I only saw him one more time in the hospital. It was the same year I got pregnant with baby number four. I was really sick. It was the pregnancy that I would miscarry. The doctor told me not to get pregnant for six months, but three months later, I was pregnant with Mark.

From the time I became a born-again Christian in 1973, I was in desperate need for God to constantly surround me with his love. I was trying to be good enough for my dad to love me. I was trying hard to be good enough for my husband to love me. It wasn't working. It was hard to reconcile in my mind that God loved me while my husband did not.

God told me once to count sand. I did. I counted about fifty thousand grains of sand in two and I half tablespoons. Psalm 139 (HCSB) says that his thoughts of love for us outnumber the grains of sand. That helped, but I wanted my husband to love me.

I misunderstood God and his ways. I had asked him to teach me his ways, and he was. It just wasn't what I had expected. It was a common misunderstanding.

I believed that if God loved me, he would rescue me from all my problems. I believed that if God loved me, he would make Fred love me. He didn't. I prayed more prayers than I can express for Fred to come to know and love God. He wasn't interested, and I must have failed, or somehow, I didn't have strong enough faith. It had to be my fault.

I lived with these thoughts of condemnation for years. I wasn't a good wife.

I had one deeper, deeper belief. That belief was that the real reason God loved me was because I tried really hard to be good. I needed to learn that, that was a lie.

For the last ten years of our marriage, our routine was Fred worked, I took care of the kids and the household, he came home for supper and then watched TV the rest of the night. I would get the kids into bed sometime between nine and ten, and then he would leave. Sometimes, I would beg him to talk to me and not leave, but he would listen silently with no response and then leave and come home a couple of hours or more later.

In those ten years, this happened every night, except a handful of times. I counted. I was so lonely, and it tormented me. I filled my life with loving my kids. I just poured all my love into them as best as I could. They were the love of my life. People would always remark about what good kids they were. I thought that it was because I was a good mother. Now I know that they were just good kids. God was kind to me—

Our generation had several idioms like "Don't throw the baby out with the bathwater," or "You married me this way, I have no intention of changing," or "Don't fix something that is not broken." I know from my heart that Fred never, ever intentionally tried to hurt me, but when you refuse to come out of your introvert world, which you are comfortable in, you can be quite surprised at what you will find. If he had taken the time to get to know his wife during those sixteen years, this could have been averted.

But to me, he was very comfortable with me functioning as his mother everywhere but the bedroom. He actually only called me *ma*—never, not even once, did I hear him call me by my name. He was not willing to come out of his comfortable world.

I was not willing to stay in it. I was fast approaching that road in the woods that Robert Frost had written about in his poem—the second one, the one less taken.

Chapter 12

James 1:14 (HCSB) reads, "But each person is tempted when he is drawn away and enticed by his own evil desires. Then after desire has conceived, it gives birth to sin, and when sin is fully grown, it gives birth to death."

As a gardener, I know that nothing grows unless there is a seed, and that seed only reproduces after its own kind. We reap what we sow.

Before I move on to the weightier stuff, I need some humor.

One of the last conversations Fred and I had before he left the house was the comment he made—he thought I was boring.

One of my dearest friends, Anne Bateman, started college around that time. She had composed a poem about me for an assignment and gave it to me years later. She has given me permission to share it.

> I have a friend
> She was potatoes and faded wallpaper
> She loved him
> Washed his socks, bore his children
> Love is a living thing
> Without nurture, it fails and dies
> My friend was lonely
> Sixteen years she waited for his love
> Sixteen years: her life turned to gray cardboard
> The love dried and fell off—
> As a flower that lost its lifeblood

> Waiting, a callous grew over her face
> Looking in a mirror, she saw nothing
> No pink cheeks
> No loveliness
> Cataracts of loneliness hide beauty
> Cardboard covers and
> Potatoes boiling, boiling to mush.

Well, maybe it is not so funny—this was written in 1985.

Since that time, I have refound the happy little girl who ran, searching through the fields for adventure. It was hard to find her back then.

To me, the humor is that she was still there—alive and well. No one saw her, but God did. He knew her well.

But, despite all that, I still have tears when I read this poem. I carried about shame that words could not express. Isaiah wrote in chapter 54, "For the Lord has called you like a wife deserted and grieved in spirit, like a wife of youth when she is cast off, says your God" (HCSB).

That was one side of my life. The other side was that I was deeply, tenderly, compassionately loved by God. He surrounded me like I was his most treasured possession. Those were the years that I learned to play guitar. I would sing to him, and he sang over me. "I am my beloved's, and he is mine. His banner over me is love."

During those years, several songs were written on my heart—songs that God wrote there. They were gifts to me. At that time, I thought of my guitar as a dear friend, one I ran to for solace. God would wake me up early in the morning, and I would get a piece of bread and my silver wine-cup and fill it with grape juice. We had communion together.

His covenant promise of love is never-ending. He is the same yesterday, today, and forever. His love rolled over me like the waves of the ocean. He was as strong and unmoving as his majestic mountains. Looking back, I am overwhelmed by God's great love.

It transcends anything we could ever dream of or hope for. I was created with the need to be loved because that is what his heart's desire for me always has been. I just didn't know it quite yet. All of the afflictions in life would soon bring about his life being established deeply in my heart so no one could ever steal it from me again.

But these things had not yet happened—that would take a few more years and a lot more pain. Pain does that. We go one way or another—we either learn or not. If we don't, the pain continues. No one wants that. I should have embraced it then, but I couldn't.

Back in those days, I had been working part-time. I found something I could do to make money and afford to put the kids into Christian school. I drove around the town, delivering the local newspapers to everyone in the tubes by the mailboxes. Either my mom would watch the kids, or I took Mark with me. I learned that I could not take Matthew because he would get carsick.

I loved driving around, doing that. One day, I had a fleeting thought and made a comment to God that, if I ever needed to work, I would love to get a job at the post office. That was early winter in the beginning of 1983. It was not a request or even a prayer. I was just talking to him. But I guess that is what prayer really is—having a conversation with God. A conversation is two people talking to each other, not a one-way street. I strongly disliked one-way conversations. It was like talking to a wall, and I had had far too many of those with Fred.

One day, something inside me felt like I should fast—so I did. At the end of three days, I didn't know why I was fasting, so I asked the Lord. Then I opened up my Bible to Isaiah chapter 58. It talks about what God is looking for when we fast. I read eagerly, searching for what he had to say. There it was.

Verse 7 says to share your bread with the hungry. I said, "God, I don't know anyone poor," which was rather funny as we were poor ourselves in many respects. But then, I thought about a family that had attended our church recently. They had a bunch of kids, maybe seven, and the father had not yet found a job. I had about $75 and went to the store. In those days, that filled at least three bags full, then I gathered up things I had at home and drove over to the place they were renting. That was very difficult for me, as I was still very insecure. I bravely knocked on their door but embarrassed, either for them or, maybe, me—yes. That was what it was. I was embarrassed for me. What if I had not really heard correctly from the Lord? That was very possible.

They opened the door. I explained that I had some things to give them, and we unloaded my car. After carrying the bags inside, they invited me in. With tears in their eyes, they told me about the prayers the family had prayed the night before. They had made a list of things they desperately needed. They asked God for these things. It was on the table before me—everything I had brought over was on that list.

They showed me their refrigerator, and it was empty. I was stunned and drove home in silence. These things have nothing to do with who we are and everything to do with who God is. I was very humbled, even to this day as I write this down.

One month later, I got a very unexpected phone call. The Maple Plain postmaster called me and asked me if I would like a job. working at the office one block from our home. I took only a second to answer. I was a close friend with his wife, who I did Bible studies with. This was nearly forty years ago. I am so overwhelmed by the love of God. I worked there for thirty-one years, never forgetting how I got there.

I had no education after high school yet ended up at a job that I just loved. My first paycheck I received back then, God said to me, "You can never outgive me."

One never can. The heart of God listens to those who love him and gives without measure. I want to be like him.

On the other hand, having my job at the post office opened up the possibility that I might no longer be financially dependent. We had no debt, and I had a real job. The seeds of freedom were stirring around in my heart. Those seeds had been sitting there dormant for a long time. Seeds will grow when they are watered.

I went to New Testament Church in Eden Prairie for about two years. I poured my heart into helping out at this school, where the kids were attending. They attended school there for four years. I paid for and put together a small library. I joined a home group and frequently lead the music with my guitar. It was a large church, and everyone came with their spouses and appeared to be so happy. Inside me, I placed myself into a caste-like system of belief that, as a woman with a husband who didn't believe, I had little or no value. I believed that my small faith was the reason Fred didn't believe. It was somehow my fault. No one put that on me. I did it myself. But at that time, I envied their marriages. I broke God's tenth commandment—do not covet.

If you haven't noticed in your own life—breaking one easily leads to breaking another.

In the Spring of 1984, one morning in church, as I sat alone. I looked down and noticed a single ant wandering around on the carpet. That morning, I had a conversation with the evil one (who is very cunning and always a liar—always eager to talk to you and deceive you). It went like this:

"Look at that poor ant. He is lost."

I said, "He is just like me!"

He replied, "Yes, you are just like that little lost ant. Why don't you rescue him?"

That was the morning that I picked up that little ant, set him outside, and decided to stop going to church and to leave my husband. I decided that, if God wasn't going to give me a husband who loved me, I would go find one myself. It was pretty easy to find a man who would talk to me.

I had told Fred earlier that if he didn't start talking to me, I would go and find someone who would. I am sure that he had not believed me, but then, he had not really paid attention. He soon did, as I gave him a month to find someplace else to live.

Everyone was in shock. My kids were crying. I loved them so very much, but my heart was so broken. The trajectory of my life would have changed completely.

If Fred had pursued me passionately—I would have stopped. He didn't.

If the pastor of my church had come and talked to me—I would have stopped. He didn't.

If Fred had tried to take the kids away from me—I would have stopped. He didn't.

I had absolutely no desire to hurt Fred. I had loved him. I was trying to stop the pain in my own heart. I am not trying to justify my decision—just telling you where I was.

It was the first time I had ever intentionally done what I knew deep in my heart was wrong. I was testing God's love for me. I needed to learn that his love carried me past my sin. Sin doesn't stop real love. Romans 8 tells us that nothing can separate us from the love of God. God never lies, even when we don't believe him.

I learned that the hard way. I thought that I was a teachable person, but apparently, I learn the hard way. Faith needs to go deep into your heart. It is not just something in your head. The heart is deceitful and desperately wicked—who can know it?

Hebrews 11:25 (KJ21) tells us that Moses chose rather to suffer affliction with the people of God than to enjoy the pleasures of sin for a season.

There is pleasure in sin for a season, but it lasts only for a season. I was really happy during this season. I had found someone else. I was really happy. I was a little girl, dancing in the fields, but that was only briefly. I would like to say a few more things.

In all of these many years, Fred and I have made sure that our children were never pulled between us. We have mutually respected each other and lived in peace, unlike the war that I had with my parents. That doesn't mean that it was easy for our children—only that we never intentionally added to the problems. I am grateful for that.

I know that Fred struggled with some of his own issues, but for some of us, we need to be in a hard place to see our need of God. I am deeply grateful that, in that whole process, he came to know Jesus as his savior. When all is said and done, that is the most important thing. I also watched as he grew up and became a loving and good father to our children. I have watched as he has become the man that God intended for him to be, and after living with him for sixteen years of my life, I am very proud of him. All this took place in 1984 and continued for the next thirteen years.

I was the prodigal daughter, with my Father watching every day for my return. He was waiting for me—patiently. He knew that I would come home.

I never stopped believing in God, and I wasn't angry at him anymore. I just left the church and my husband. I never felt God looking at me with disdain or condemnation. He was just quietly waiting. I felt his gentleness and his love for me, even when I was running from him and sinning in my heart. Many other people pointed the finger and brought condemnation. I don't blame them. I can only say with assurance that those who did, didn't see me or the pain in my heart.

The very most important lesson that I learned was that God didn't love me because I was good. He loved me because he loved me. He loved me, but he loved me enough to not leave me in my sin. The wages of sin is always death. That is not his heart's desire for us.

Chapter 13

John 15:13 reads, "No one has greater love than this, that someone would lay down his life for his friends" (HCSB).

Proverbs 18:24b (ESV) reads, "There is a friend who sticks closer than a brother."

My late twenties were the period in my life where I formed my inner circle of friends. They came from the house church we attended called El Shaddai. There was a bond that was formed during those years that has endured, despite the fact that the church did not. These friends are gold to me.

I have many friends that I dearly love, but these I would have to call the inner circle. They have faithfully loved me throughout all of my wildness and failures.

In the center of this circle would be Barb. I am not sure what others do without a faithful, God-loving friend like Barb. She carried me faithfully in all of my dark years. She never let me forget who I was. She walked wisely and gently through the valley of the shadow of death with me, holding my hand as often as I would let her. She cherished me.

A good friend sees the good in your heart, when no one else does. They do not look at the moments of your failures; they see the future and believe in you.

She remembered the songs that God gave me and sang them in her heart when I was no longer singing them. We will be friends throughout eternity. One does not earn a friend like this. You never could, but I know who gave her to me.

Barb, Steve, and I would play guitars and lead worship. I loved music. It soothed my soul and brought great comfort. We all wrote songs that came from our hearts and eagerly taught them to the fellowship. Being part of a team was healing to my soul. We would have Bible studies, and we had times of great laughter. I was so serious that it was good for me to laugh. One time at Bible study, Barb looked down and pointed out that the sock I had on my foot was a sock that Michelle had made a puppet out of. It had ears and a face.

Barb and I would record the songs that we wrote on a tape recorder (which we used all the time back then). We passed them on to others to teach the songs. One time, when we listened to what we had recorded, there was her bulldog, Max, snoring in the background. I cherish these memories. Thank you, Barb, for loving me.

Chapter 14

Hosea 2:6–7, 14 (NASB) reads:

> Therefore, behold, I will obstruct her way with thorns, and I will build a stone wall against her so that she cannot find her paths. And she will pursue her lovers, but she will not reach them; and she will seek them, but will not find them—I am going to persuade her, bring her into the wilderness, and speak kindly to her.

It was not hard to find a man. Breaking away from my chains brought about things that I am not proud of. I thought about writing these things down, but it really is unnecessary, and later, I would deeply repent of my behavior. I am forgiven. There is no depth of sin God will not forgive from a humble broken heart.

But I was still on the search to be loved, and that would bring my second husband into my life. I was no longer an eighteen-year-old, and I deeply loved my second husband. He was handsome, charming, generous, and a hard worker. He liked to have fun with the kids, and especially, Michael loved him. He told me that he was a Christian, and I believed that he was backslidden like me and he would return to the Lord—like I knew I would. As a very honest person, I was naïve to think that all people are honest as well. I believed everything he said.

I shouldn't have. We dated for two years, and I watched closely for warning signs of things I couldn't live with. He didn't smoke or drink or do porn or appear to have a temper or watch sports or anything on my list of no-nos. He had really good stories of all the ways his life had been hard and how he had overcome and persevered. He was the king of his very dysfunctional family—the only person, to that point, in his family who had made it through high school and wasn't living on welfare. He was highly respected by his family and the community. He had even attended the nearby Christian college, though he had flunked out.

I had found what I had been searching for. We married on September 23, 1988. That lasted for fifteen years. For the first year, things proceeded on the surface as they had while we had dated. Then out of the blue, he was angry with me.

I cowered and was stunned and afraid. For the rest of the years, his anger appeared almost every week. I stood between him and the kids as a shield. If I went a month without him being angry, I thought I was in heaven. I just tried all the harder to be a good wife. He was always having trouble with his kids and ex-wife. He always played the martyr. I knew nothing about people who were narcissists. Our marriage was all about him. He had great value, and I was fortunate to be his wife. He loved doing things for others so that that he could feel like they owed him.

I was terribly afraid that this marriage would not make it. I was holding on to him fiercely. He was not holding on to me. The only thing that he ever told me I was good at was being a mother. That was a lie. He told me that I wanted things that I was never going to get. That was not true either. God does not put things into your heart that he doesn't want to give you.

Good things came out of those years: I learned that I loved to travel, I learned that I loved to quilt, I learned that I loved to garden. I learned a lot.

God works *all* things together for good.

Out of the blue one day, God wrote a new song on my heart. It was from Romans 8:28:

> Behold, all things work together for good. Behold all things work together for good, for the chil-

dren of the heavenly Father—behold all things, work together for good.

Unto them that trust His mercy; unto them who love His name; unto them the promise given—behold all things work together for good.

Looking back on it, that must have been the time that I began to miss walking with God. I wanted to come back, but I didn't know how. God began a two-year plan of making a way where there was no way—for his daughter to come home. It was ingenious.

Deep inside, I knew there was a choice I had to make—God or my husband. Yet I hoped that he would make peace with God and our marriage would heal. I tried to talk to him about God, but that would make him angry. Like me when I was young, he thought what he had was being a Christian, but the fruit of his life never showed it. A tree is always known by its fruit. Don't be deceived. I would never have left him unless he started physically abusing my kids. I had warned him once about Mark. But I still had hope that he would return to God. He didn't. God was clearly telling me that he would have no other idols before him. I idolized my husband and pretty much kissed his toes. There was danger ahead.

Michelle graduated from college and lived at home for a while. She was very good at saving money, and an opportunity was placed in our pathway. An older woman on my mail route had passed away, and the Hennepin County Park District was going to burn the house down. It was an awesome house, and the plan opened up to buy it and move it off Park property. It was so much work, but there was great excitement that she could have a home for a reasonable price. I had fears of the kids ever being able to afford homes as prices seemed so outrageous. (That is funny, considering prices today!) We worked hard, finding a moving company, finding land we could put it on, cutting down countless trees to clear the path—the issues were endless.

I was excited! We did so many things in our younger years. Life was always busy. Life was about the kids. I wanted them to be happy and do well in life. I never, for a moment, wanted them to struggle with the things I had to deal with. Maybe I didn't tell them enough how very—how deeply—I loved them. I don't know. I am not sure. I should have done better.

The night we moved, the house was a warm early December night, and the house was lit up like a Christmas tree. There were railroad tracks we had to cross and streetlights that had to be moved. I would never move a house again but wouldn't have missed this experience. Later, the family would thank us for rescuing the house. There was still so much work to do once we moved it.

Everyone helped Michelle. One of the movers was a very charming and attractive young man. I am not going into that story, but he would become the father of my two oldest grandchildren. The pathway home to God was around the bend, as God had used the death of Paul back in 1972 to push me toward him—death would send me sobbing and running back to him again.

Drunk with alcohol, John would accidentally discharge a gun killing the guy he was with. He hurried back from up North to her house and fell asleep, not telling her what had happened. She found her home surrounded by the police, and John went to jail.

We both went running back to God. I sobbed for a month and started attending a new church Barb had found. Things were going to change in my marriage. I repented with all my heart. I had lost so many years of time with the Lord. He took me back like I was his dearly beloved daughter. He had been watching for me and had made a way where there had been no way. Salvation is not what we do for God—it is all about what he does to rescue us from ourselves. We are lost, and he runs after us—he makes a way. We run; he runs after us.

I knew that in those thirteen years, I had lost much. I hurt my children that I love so much. I had lost some of the other gifts God had given me. I couldn't remember many of the songs God had given to me in the early years.

In tears, as I was mourning these things, one day on my mail route, I asked God if he would please give me one more song. I was startled as he began to do just that. By the time I was done with my route that day, I was singing a new song.

LET THE MORNING BRING ME WORD

> Oh Lord, you are holy, and we are your children,
> For you have redeemed us and called us your own.
> We love and adore you; we bow down before you,
> And all of our days, we will sing of your praise.
> Jesus our savior, the Lord God almighty,
> Our rock, our redeemer—the lamb that was slain,
> The light of the world, the way to the Father—
> Humbled and broken—
> Emmanuel

I prayed all the more for my husband.

It is not that God didn't answer my prayers. He now was going to rescue me from more than myself. I was not prepared for his plan. But he knows what is best for us. What he does is not always what we would choose. He wasn't giving me a choice. He stood between my husband and me and removed me from this marriage. He is a jealous God, and idols need to go. My husband left on his own accord.

Chapter 15

Matthew 7:17, 20 (HCSB) reads, "Every good tree produces good fruit, but a bad tree produces bad fruit—so you'll recognize them by their fruit."

Making plans for our lives without God is always unwise. Some things are redeemed; some are not.

His first granddaughter was born in December of 2001. I just loved her more than words could say. It was that mother thing in me, and she was and is special. I was close with his daughter-in-law and was allowed to take Alyssa almost every weekend from an early age. I loved her and always will.

I had also become close to several of his family members and had the privilege of leading two of the nieces in the prayer of salvation. They were very needy, and I did my best to share God's love with them. I didn't even know what the word narcissist meant but have learned that they don't like to share the spotlight with others.

The last year of our marriage brought about heart health issues with him and the focus of our attention was on that. Life was always about him, and I had become accustomed to that. But when some of the tests came up negative and counseling was suggested, he wanted no part of that. The doctor then prescribed some type of sedative. Drugs will never cure sin. They only cover stuff up. The truth will set you free, but often, we love our sin, and the darkness is where it breeds.

Christmas of 2002 was our last. Once in a blue moon, something prophetic comes out of my mouth—totally unintended but it comes out nonetheless. I was thinking about Alyssa and innocently said, "Now I have to share his heart with another woman."

He must have gone into shock at that moment, but as many people do, the surface covers up truth—what is really underneath. God always knows what is in our hearts. We can lie to ourselves and others, but God sees it all.

Come Valentine's Day, there was an excuse to go visit his brother in Fergus Falls. He had a beautiful bouquet of flowers sent to my workplace, along with the most romantic card he had ever given to me. I was thrilled. I thought we had gotten past some rough spots and things were better. I cleaned the house up really good and eagerly waited for him to get home. He came home in a fit of rage. I went into shock.

I didn't understand that there was an intentional plan to start creating problems to deflect what was really going on. He knew that I was afraid of anger and it would throw me off track. He became angry about everything and looked for fights.

I have come to understand that a liar lies, a martyr must always look for sympathy, and a narcissist will never yield to anything that stands in their way of getting what they want and think they deserve. If he had just said, "I don't love you anymore and want out," I would have sadly given him what he wanted, but that would have disrupted his martyr role and our property would have been divided equally between us. But that was not what was fair in his mind.

There was no intentions of equal division, and I knew where all the money was. It would be a long time before anyone would believe he was having an affair. He would never do that, would he? He even convinced his attorney for a long time. He was very good at that kind of stuff—making himself look innocent. That's what martyrs do.

I actually went into deep shock. There were times that I had trouble breathing. I literally felt the Holy Spirit helped me breathe. It felt like my heart had broken into a million pieces—shattered, and it had no chance of ever being whole again.

He played around with this stuff for a while and tried to make me think there was hope. I prayed so hard—so hard. I sobbed and sobbed to the Lord. I forgave him and begged God to rescue him from his sin. Love does that. I didn't know that God was rescuing me.

On his side, he was calling friends of mine and telling them his plan to trick me. He didn't know that it would come back to me. I had been saving up money to take us to Hawaii on vacation for his birthday. Instead, I shifted money, paid off my car loan, and went to Hawaii by myself.

My three weeks in Hawaii were the most wonderful time I had ever had in my entire life up to that point. God just poured out his love like a flood. I heard him in everything that I did. I worshipped him. There was joy everywhere. It was the first time I didn't have to do anything to take care of anyone.

It was hard to explain. My sister came and spent the middle week with me. Michelle's mother-in-law lived on Maui and was so kind to let me stay with her and use her car. I will be forever grateful for her kindness. I needed it.

I still had hope. I called him on my birthday, and my birthday present was his announcement—he was filing for divorce. Happy birthday. That didn't steal my joy.

I hiked up into the mountains and spent the night by a waterfall. God loved me—that was all that mattered. I learned that the music in the streams was not just created by the water. It came from the water, rushing over the rocks.

I learned that God doesn't always remove the rocks. It is their presence that causes the song to be sung. I was starting to learn the ways of God. There were more lessons before I really understood, but it was the beginning.

I went home and prepared myself for a divorce. I thought it would be easy. He was preparing for war and had hired an older female attorney. He was good at manipulating women.

I hired an attorney that my pastor's wife had recommended, supposedly a Spirit-filled man. I say supposedly because I would later learn that he was as dishonest as the rest of them—actually, worse as he claimed to be a Christian. That tricked me too. I was walking into a minefield. I would eventually call this the divorce from hell—there was evil everywhere, and it caught me off guard. To be honest, the darkness all around me frightened me deeply—shocked me—and I took my eyes off of Jesus.

In 2004, I started seeing my postmaster. It distracted me. He was eager to help me with mowing and things I was not used to doing.

There had been a threat to burn down the marital house, so I put in an alarm system. My husband broke in with that, so I got a restraining order against him. He hired a criminal defense attorney, and my attorney counseled me to agree to a mutual restraining order. I believed him. I thought that the divorce was going to end the spring of 2004, so I bought a house in Rockford. I knew the marital house would need to be sold. Both attorneys didn't want it to end, as there was money to be harvested, and both put an end to settling. I was told that I had to go to trial.

Larry helped me by moving into the house, as two houses were way more than I could carry. In December 2004, my attorney handed me a bill for $100,000 for the month of November. I went into shock. Shortly after that, my beloved uncle Gene had a stroke and went into a nursing home in Wisconsin. I thought he was going to die. I rushed to Wisconsin and spent time there. I was doing a huge amount of work for the divorce, and Larry had a better computer at the house in Rockford, so I was up many nights, working on that.

While I was there, the furnace went out at the marital house. When I went home, I found the water pipes broken and water gushing from the upstairs bathroom all the way down to the basement. I didn't even know how to turn off the well. There was $30,000 worth of damage to the house. The judge gave the house to my husband and gave me two weeks to move out. It was winter, and moving things while trying to work was not easy. The employees at work became angry. Larry tried to comfort me by taking me on a trip to Mexico, only to crash on a rented moped the second day. We rushed home with his broken collarbone, cracked rib, cracked hip bone, and bruises all over.

It was all I could take. The pressure was on, and my only place of comfort was that I knew God loved me. I wanted to go home to be with him. I had never before thought about suicide, but it sounded like a way of escaping this very real pain. The snowball was rolling quickly downhill. I told my daughter and pastor that I didn't want to be here anymore.

Then God spoke. All he said was, "Your grandchildren need you."

That stopped me in my tracks. I only had one at that time, but God never says things he doesn't mean, and I would soon learn that I had three more grandchildren on the way. Eventually, I would have eight. I will be eternally grateful to God for saying what I needed to hear to stop me.

I just love my grandchildren. In April of 2005, God put an end to it all, and there was a settlement for the same amount that I had tried to get my attorney to offer back in late 2003. That was after attorney bills on both sides had run up to $250,000. This trial was the last my attorney ever handled. He was later disbarred and had felony charges for stealing his client's property. I didn't pay him the last $20,000, and he spent the next three years adding illegal interest until it reached $50,000. He sued me and lost. He took it to appeals court and lost. He finally took me to the Minnesota Supreme Court and lost.

I gained a terror of the court system, as, during the divorce, I witnessed major corruption—attorneys and judges alike. When all of this ended, the judge, my husband's attorney, my attorney, and my ex-husband all suffered from major health issues and went on disability. God sees it all. He offers to everyone a lifeline to rescue them from their sins. It is not his desire that we die in our sins. My hope is that, before it is too late, they all take his lifeline. That is my hope and prayer. It would take time to forgive them, but unforgiveness hurts the one holding on to it. I didn't need any more pain.

I heard an old saying that pain is God's megaphone to a deaf world. I couldn't agree more.

From this point on, my new saying was, "Life didn't start when my husband came into my life, and it wasn't going to end when he was gone." Life is too short to let the sins of others leave you without hope. That was never going to happen.

I do want to say one more thing about all of this—one of the last things my ex-husband said to deeply hurt me was he told my youngest son that it was all his fault. I want it on record that it was *never, ever* his fault. Sin always deflects and blames others.

When we point the finger at someone else, there are always four fingers pointing back at us.

God is just, and revenge is not our responsibility. God is not just a loving God, there is wrath to come in the end if there is no repentance.

But after visiting all of this, I am tired and need a break—

Chapter 16

Psalm 103:13–14 (ESV) reads, "As a father shows compassion to his children, so the Lord shows compassion to those who fear Him. For He knows our frame; He remembers that we are dust."

As I think about my mother, I think of the song "Jesus Loves Me."

There is the line that says, "We are weak, but he is strong. Yes, Jesus loves me." That was my mom. I am overwhelmed by the mercy of God and his compassion toward those who belong to him. It is never about us. It is about him alone.

When I think of Mom, I also think of the old picture of footprints in the sand. A man had a dream of his life, and during many times of his life, he saw two sets of footprints then, at times, saw only one set of footprints.

Asking God why he had abandoned him in the hard times, God replied, "I never abandoned you. The one set of footprints was me carrying you."

That was my mother too.

To tell her story, I am going to go backward—the end, the middle, and the beginning of her walk with the Lord. She ended so well. I am so proud of her.

My mother spent the last independent years of her life in an income-based apartment very near where I worked. Those were the years and time that our hearts healed, and we had let go of the things that had come between us. She loved my visits and stopped trying to make me feel guilty for not giving her more time. We laughed and played Skip-Bo every time.

In August of 2013, she got sick with an infection and needed to go into the hospital. She needed meds and supervision for ten days, so she agreed to go temporarily into the nursing home two blocks from my workplace.

At the end of ten days, she wanted to stay (first miracle), as she liked all the attention, which was fine. It was a Christian-based home, and they were good to her. I spent a couple of weeks emptying out her apartment, as she was still a hoarder. I filled the giant dumpster more than once and the recycling containers over and over.

She liked collecting plastic for some reasons. I was amazed that she never once asked about all her stuff that she had clung to for so many years. That was the second miracle. God is always in our steps when we walk with him. Towards the end of the year, she asked me when she was going home. I told her that this was her home until she went to heaven. She accepted that peacefully.

In January, she looked at me and said, "You know, I never cry."

I knew that was true. I had not seen her cry for at least twenty years.

I replied, "That's all right, Mom. I cry enough for the both of us."

She just patted my hand. She stopped eating solid foods at that point. The nursing home told me people can live a long time on fluids and supplements.

The beginning of April, I noticed that she must have had a small stroke, as she wasn't responding as she had normally.

I had been informing my brother periodically of her condition, even though he had refused to speak to me for years. It was the right thing to do. There was silence. He had only seen her once in eight years. I offered him a place to stay and a car to use. There was still silence, of course, but I will always be glad that I did the right thing. Apparently, he decided to come, and he visited her one weekend. He left his music recorder and a picture he had taken of the two of them. She was smiling. It was a cute picture.

She turned eighty-eight on May 8, 2014. That was the day when my youngest granddaughter came into the world. She was very early and weighed under three pounds. My mother was dying, and my granddaughter was in the NICU.

I was visiting my mom twice a day—before and after work at this time. She loved me to sing to her. The last week of her life, she had not opened her eyes, but she knew my voice and squeezed my hand. I sang to her the morning of May 19 and told her I would see her after work. I will say with deep gratitude that if you are listening, you can hear the whisper of God and see his miraculous and unseen footprints—the footprints of God's presence. He was there that day.

His ways are beautiful. What happened took away any apprehension of death that I might have had. I got a call at work around 9:30. My mom had passed.

Here is the story—a young attendant had come into her room. She watched as my mother opened her eyes, which she had not for over a week, and tears began to roll down her cheeks, as she looked up into the corner of the ceiling (remember, she had not cried in twenty years), and then she was gone.

Mom saw something that young attendant hadn't. She saw eternity with the one who loved her along her journey and came to take her home.

Thank you, Lord Jesus. It was pouring rain that day. The rain hid my tears.

On the day we had her memorial service at my home, we only invited her longtime friends of twenty years or so and family. Only her son, his children, my sister's children, and her brother were absent.

That day, my flowering crab tree in the backyard flowered beautifully.

It was late to bloom—it waited for her.

Chapter 17

The middle of Mom's story that I am going to share is something that I wrote back at the end of 2013 and recorded on a CD at church as a testimony of God's faithfulness and help with difficult issues in our lives. It will tell the story better than I could do today.

This was what I wrote back then:

My mother was the second child born to my grandparents back on May 8, 1926. A third child was aborted with a coat hanger.

When my mom was eight years old, my grandmother abandoned them. My great uncle Charlie would tell me later that he was there the day his sister left and how my mom stood in the driveway and cried as she watched her go.

My mom became a Christian when I was very young, but Dad left her for another woman when I was fourteen. She never really recovered. She was rejected by a second person that she loved and needed. She cried for ten years. When she stopped crying, she became self-absorbed, difficult, and very verbal.

At fourteen, I somehow took on the mother role and felt responsible for her. Interestingly, her middle name is Marie, which means "bitter," but the spiritual connotation means "console." I tried to console her. I did that for years, but almost every conversation would lead to her talking about my dad. She had never known who she was without him.

I did everything I could think of to help her. Nothing seemed to bring the needed healing. She wanted something from me that I couldn't give her, and after more than twenty-five years of this, I became angry and very frustrated with her. I went to counseling and learned to set some healthy boundaries, which made her even more unhappy. She would talk about me to everyone, trying to find a way to get me back to where she wanted me to be.

I spent most of my life feeling as though I was a terrible daughter. I felt guilty because the Bible tells us, "Honor your father and mother." I carried this around like a heavy sack.

It effected my relationship with God because I was guilty. I was the child of abandonment and bitterness. What did that make me? Like a modern-day caste system. I came from a place of brokenness and pain. I didn't deserve more. At birth, I was given the name Linda.

For many years, I thought that God had given me the wrong name because it means "beautiful."

One day, I learned what God thought. I found a scripture in Isaiah 61, which says that God will give us "beauty for ashes." What a merciful exchange—we give him our ashes, and he gives us beauty.

I spent my life trying to forgive, but it was a constant battle that I wrestled with.

I prayed for help continually. A few years back, I went to a women's encounter at my church, which helped me release this to the Lord again. After that, something broke in the spirit, and I was able to visit my mom on a regular basis, and there was peace between us. I was able to truly forgive her and was relieved and so thankful for what God had done.

That would have been enough for me, but it wasn't for God.

Mom told me that, all of her life, she would never go into a nursing home. I had great fears about this issue, but God told me not to worry about the end of her life. I chose to believe him.

Recently, she fell and ended up in the hospital. She needed to go into a nursing home to finish her medication. At that point, she knew she couldn't live on her own anymore. She made her choice to stay there. It was a miracle.

But God had still more for me. I cleaned out her apartment and began sorting through her pictures. It was at that point that I joined a class about telling your story. I felt lead to scrapbook and collage about my early childhood. During that process, the Holy

Spirit began to show me that, when I was young, my mother did love and take care of me (us).

When I was six, our home burned down to the ground, and God showed me that Mom went back into the house while it was burning and grabbed my teddy bear and all the photos of us. God had her grab these things so that many years later, he could prove to me that I was loved, not only by him but by my mom.

It has been a long journey, but God has truly healed my heart and helped me to learn to honor my mother. God didn't make a mistake in who my parents were. He created me to help those in need, and my mother just happened to be one of them. I now thank God for her and feel deeply loved by her. I can now see that she gave me many gifts. God understands our deepest pain and is there to carry us through. He will use the hardest parts of our lives to produce beauty out of the ashes.

The scriptures say in Isaiah 53 (KJV):

> He was despised and rejected of men, a man of sorrows and acquainted with grief—surely, he hath borne our griefs, and carried our sorrows. He was wounded for our transgressions, He was bruised for our iniquities: the chastisement of our peace was upon Him, and with his stripes we are healed. All we like sheep have gone astray, we have turned everyone to his own way; and the Lord laid on him the iniquity of us all.

And in Isaiah 63 (KJV), it says:

> He became their Savior. In all their afflictions He was afflicted. And the Angel of His Presence saved them; in His love and in His pity, He redeemed them; and he lifted them and carried them all the days of old.

LINDA WASSON

    I would like to end this story about my mother with a poem she wrote in her younger years. My mom always tried to get me to read her poems, but I couldn't. I feared that they were all about her woe concerning my father. I spent my whole younger years being torn between them and did not need any fuel to flame the fire. I couldn't read them until she was gone. I was surprised.
    Here is my favorite one:

> I have a gift from my Father above,
> Wrapped in his mercy, his grace, and his love.
> Compassionate love compelled him to do:
> This wonderful deed for me and for you.
> He is a wonderful friend to me,
> Truest and dearest that 'ere could be.
> He paid for my sins and set me free,
> This friend of all friends, my savior is he
> Oh, the price of my sins, my penalty,
> Sent Jesus to die on that cruel tree.
> Oh, how my heart grieves when I think that there,
> 'twas my sins that caused him that burden to bear
> Not only that, he did so much more,
> In heaven above, beyond that great door,
> A place he prepared for one such as I,
> To dwell by his side in the sweet by and by.
> Until that great day I have inside,
> His gift of love to lead and to guide.
> For a bit of heaven now dwells within,
> To lead his child from the path of sin.
> Oh, how can I ever repay this debt,
> That Jesus my savior so willingly met.
> Oh, Lord give me strength thy will to do,
> All of the things that you want me to.
> And though I have failed him time after time,
> I know I am kept by his grace divine.
> For he knows in my weakness, I long to be true,
> That I'm sorry for all of the wrong things that I do.

> What a wonderful, wonderful friend that is he,
> So willing to bear all my sins for me.
> And by his love and grace divine,
> I know I am his, and he is mine.

I know that there was never anyone who ever prayed more for my father to come to know Jesus as his personal savior than my mom—not one.

In the end, my sister prayed with him. I don't know if my mom was surprised to see him when he left this earth, but I know she was happy and know it was worth it all.

Today, she is with my little daughter that I lost in a miscarriage many years ago. Her name is Joy.

In my imagination, I wonder if she looks like me. Maybe she does—

Chapter 18

Psalm 63:3 (AMP) reads, "Your lovingkindness is better than life."

The story of my life could never be complete without giving space to honor the two people I would come to consider my third set of parents. God's great kindness to me in filling up those gaps in my life that my birth parents could never fill went beyond kindness—it was truly loving-kindness. I never closed my heart off or walled myself into a place where I couldn't see opportunities for people to love and be loved by.

Around late 1990, I heard that my uncle Gene and aunt Lou had moved to Wisconsin and had become believers in Jesus Christ. I had hardly spent time with them when I was young, but I knew I had been named after him. Everyone loved Uncle Gene.

I invited them to come to our home for Thanksgiving, and they came that year. Our hearts became bound together from that point on. They were my God-loving, praying parents. I adored them and knew that they loved me. If you called them on the phone and got their answering machine, you would hear Uncle Gene say, "We want you to know that Jesus loves you, and so do we."

They lived their lives well. Uncle Gene was the kindest and gentlest man I have ever known. Aunt Lou was a sassy, spunky, cute little thing, and Uncle Gene loved her with all of his heart. I miss them deeply—

Aunt Lou went home to be with Jesus in June of 2017, the year that I lost five people that I loved. I was not there, but I am comforted in my soul because of what happened.

I was visiting them at the time that the people who were managing her daily care were trying to get Gene to understand that bringing in hospice would be a good decision for them both. I had just gone through hospice with the passing of my husband and knew that it was a good thing. My assurance helped him to make that decision. He called Brenda that night and told her of the decision. She had a flight scheduled for a couple of weeks out, but because of hospice, she changed her flight and flew out right away. I went home, but Brenda got to be with her mother the last week or so of her life. She was there when her mother passed. It was all good. Brenda was always a wonderful daughter.

Uncle Gene would leave us on March 17, 2018, one year to the exact date that my dad died. I was the last one in the family to see him and kiss him and tell him that I loved him.

I wrote my own memorial for each of them after they passed on—these writings are the best expression of their impact on my life, so that is what I choose to leave in honoring them. I will see them again someday when my days are finished here on earth.

In honor of my aunt Lou—

I have always loved my aunts. I have no idea why God was so kind to me and gave me so many of them. He must have known that I needed them so much. I can only state how deeply grateful I am—to them and to God.

Every good and perfect gift comes down from the Father, my loving Father, who never changes.

My first aunt who deeply impacted my life was Aunt Rosemary. As a young child, she pulled the family together and always hugged me. I always desperately needed her hugs and smiles. Thank you, Aunt Rosemary.

When I was a teenager and my parents divorced, my aunt Eunice took me into her home and let me live with them. For forty years, I traveled to Grand Rapids because I knew it was a place where I was loved. She passed away while I was visiting in Montana—all plans stopped as I drove straight through to attend the funeral. I wasn't her real daughter, but I was. I loved her.

As I became older, my aunt Phyllis became very dear to me. We traveled together, and she helped me make peace with my father. I was hoping to have her in my life for a few more years, as she was the youngest, but that didn't happen.

That brings me to Aunt Lou—what can I say?

Though Brenda has always been her beloved daughter, I gladly took my place, as an adopted second daughter. There was a bond between Lou and me.

Aunt Lou was a mom to me. Gene and Lou always prayed for me. I knew that—always. Their love and prayers were a gift to me from God. They never made me feel guilty if I hadn't called for a while. No matter what kind of chaos there was in my life (and there was plenty of it), I knew I could talk to them about it, and after they were done, I was at peace and laughing again. Thank you, Aunt Lou and Uncle Gene, for your wisdom, patience, forgiveness, and prayers. Thank you for your love, which helped me so much and changed my life for the good. You have been a precious gift to me. There was always an unspoken vow in my heart that I would make that three-and-a-half-hour trip from Minnesota several times a year until their last breath.

My life has been blessed with riches that no money could ever buy. People who love are like treasures of gold, silver, and precious jewels. We can miss that wealth if our hearts are not open.

I wouldn't have missed knowing you for all the world. I love you, Aunt Lou—

Uncle Gene's memorial. It is very appropriate that Brenda picked this weekend to have her dad's memorial, as it is Father's Day weekend. Uncle Gene was a good father.

I know that the thing he would have me say is, "The most important thing all of us need is to know our heavenly Father!"

It is ultimately the greatest need in this life. Jesus himself was utterly dependent on his Father—his Father and ours if we are born again. But God the Father is a Spirit, and as human beings, we tend to look at what is seen or our earthly fathers. They are supposed to be a kind of mirror reflection of what our heavenly Father is like. Many times, our earthly fathers do not reflect him accurately. This inaccurate reflection can bring confusion. It did to me.

I can say that, without a doubt, Uncle Gene and Aunt Lou prayed for everyone in the family—that they would come to know Jesus.

In 1990, Uncle Gene and Aunt Lou came into my life. They loved me, and I loved them. Brenda was kind enough to share her parents with me. I could never be a good daughter that she always was, but I was thankful to be their second daughter. They reflected the heavenly Father's heart. They were always patient and kind and faithfully loved me. They always prayed for me, and I am eternally grateful.

I was in Arizona for a month when Uncle Gene went on hospice. I prayed that I could see him one more time. I arrived home late March 15. We couldn't come until Saturday, and as we had started on the road for our trip there, Uncle Gene called and told me he wasn't feeling too well and, maybe, I shouldn't come. I told him we were coming anyway.

Before we got there, the nurse strongly told him he should go to the hospital.

His response was, "I can't. I have company coming."

He was waiting for me. I knew it.

After we got there, he called Brenda and talked to her. He always called you *sweetie*. Then the ambulance was called. I hugged him and kissed him and told him that I loved him. It was a precious moment that I cherish. Thank you, God.

Almost sixty-seven years ago, a little girl was born, and her parents named her Linda Jean Burgan. Jean was after her dad's youngest brother. I carry his name proudly.

Thank you, Uncle Gene, for being a good reflection of God the Father. I am now ready to have only one Father—

Chapter 19

First John 3:1 (ESV) reads, "See what kind of love the Father has given to us, that we should be called children of God; and so, we are."

My father was the firstborn in his family, followed by Dennis, Gene, Betty, and Phyllis.

In the Spring of 2013, my sister and I took a trip up to Side Lake, Minnesota, with him to visit the area that he grew up in. It was beautiful. We drove to several places while he reminisced about his childhood. He grew up in the depression, and their family was very poor.

The boys learned to hunt at an early age, which was something he would love for the rest of his life. They also got into mischief as three brothers tend to do. Work was scarce, and his mom and the kids were left for long periods to fend for themselves.

They lived in a very small shack-type house, while the in-laws lived next door, quite well-off and, according to Aunt Phyllis, were not exactly loving grandparents.

I don't know how old my dad was when my grandmother contracted tuberculosis, and the kids were split up between foster homes. My father had not yet finished high school.

My dad was separated from his siblings, while the younger boys were kept together and the girls were kept together. That was the end of family life for my father. He would marry my mother in 1945, at the age of eighteen, and somewhere in there, he briefly join the Navy, which he strongly disliked, as he never tolerated anyone telling him what to do.

In 2010, shortly after the passing of my stepmother, he told my sister and me that the family he had spent time with when his mother was sick was in fact a very nice family who treated him well, but they were what he called Holy Rollers.

For the first time in my life, I realized that his hatred of religious people did not start with my mother. I was shocked, as I had blamed my mother all those years.

My father was a handsome man when he was young, as were his brothers and sisters. They were all easygoing the years that I knew them. My dad's two brothers would grow up to be wonderful husbands and fathers and loved their children. I could never understand why my father wasn't anything like them. He was in many ways like his own father.

I set out, determined to make my dad love me. He was a perfectionist. I tried to be perfect for him, but early in my life, I learned that I couldn't. I was aware that I was the favorite of both of my parents, but being his favorite only meant that he found some pride, which reflected on him in some way. It wasn't love. The little daddy's girl chased him all of his life, searching for some kind of genuine love. I would drive from Minnesota every year to see him. He never, not even once, came my way for thirteen years.

When his wife inherited some money, they bought a piece of property in Wisconsin near his two brothers. I was so excited that my dad was going to live closer to me. So my second husband and I bought two acres on a river in Wisconsin not far away. I dreamed in later years that he would be close by. I was heartbroken again, as he up and pulled their possessions to Wyoming because he wasn't going to let his neighbors tell him what he could do with his property. He didn't even tell me, so that balloon popped as well.

I would drive to Colorado to see him, and he wouldn't be there, even after I told him I was coming. He did stop at my home twice later on in the years. I was so excited that my dad was there. I got up early in the morning to spend some time with him, and both times, he was already gone without a word. My heart was broken over and over. Yet I still longed for his affection. I never heard my dad say one kind thing about my brother, and though my sister had spent her high school years with him, they had offended each other and barely spoke for almost fifty years. I tried to be the peacemaker and would drag her over to his place on several occasions to little avail.

They were both stubborn, and until my stepmother passed away in 2010, my sister would tell me that she had no feelings or affection for Dad. My mom often said that the opposite of love was never hate—it was indifference. That was practiced in my family. The only person that I ever saw my dad love, besides himself, was my stepmother. They were together for forty-five years. I take that back—he loved my great uncle Charlie and his brother Gene. My uncle Charlie loved him too—but was very grieved at my dad's lack of love for his children. Maybe that is why my uncle Charlie loved me so very much—he could see the pain. That is the way life was. One might say that he wasn't a drunk or abusive physically or sexually or verbally or whatever, and I agree that those things are terrible. But emotional abandonment is emotional abuse and brings far more destruction than the world wants to talk about. One only needs to look at the long-term effect of it on my family of origin. It creates an inability to bond, and it travels through the generations.

My dad was always healthy, and we expected him to live well into his nineties. He would always say that the most important thing was the ability to walk, and if you couldn't walk, you might as well shoot yourself. The first two years after my stepmother died, I had his attention. He was struggling out in Wyoming. I wrote him many letters and sent packages every month, and for the first time, he would say, "I love you—don't you know?"

It was the first time I believed it. Those were sweet moments. He would call me his pretty little girl. I can't say that I didn't love it. He was eighty-three when Carna passed away, and I traveled out there often with my sister from that point. We didn't know it, but dementia was creeping up on him. He had always prided himself in the fact that he was so smart and needed no one. My mom had prayed for him for years, and God was bringing about some necessary humility.

I had encouraged Dad to come visit not only us but his brothers in Wisconsin as well. He didn't tell me that he set out to do that very thing. Two days later, I got a phone call from Aunt Rosemary. My dad was seven hours south of me with a kind farmer, who had found him in his cornfield all confused. He didn't know where he was and believed that he was by Uncle Gene's home. Something was seriously wrong. I left around midnight to go rescue my dad.

They had fed him and tucked him into bed for the night. That morning, he was surprised to find me there and determined to visit his brothers, even though he had no idea where he was. Well, his family had much experience with Alzheimer's and dementia and had enough of their own physical problems going on in Wisconsin.

Dad was furious that he was not welcome there at that time. I tried to get my dad to come stay at my home for a day or two before he returned home, but he would have no part of that. I just thought that he was exhausted. I rode with him to US Highway 90 as he turned west to go home. He would not go home on 80 because he had spent two days confused and lost on it.

I called him repeatedly, expecting him to be home. He wasn't. I was out to dinner when I got the phone call that dad was in the hospital in Laramie. He had found himself way too far north in Wyoming and needed to find his way south. A nice policeman showed him a place he could sleep in his car for the night. The next morning, he was traveling the wrong direction on the freeway. A policeman stopped him and helped him get in the correct lane to go south.

When Dad got to US 80, he headed west toward Laramie. He couldn't remember what exit to take and followed a semi down an exit. He was standing confused at a gas station, when he was spotted by another policeman. Dad's plates were run, and it was found that he had been stopped earlier that morning. The policeman questioned him. He told them that he was just coming back from a hunting trip in the mountains. He told them he had no family or friends who would come and get him. So they put his dog in the dog pound, impounded his truck, and put him in a locked unit in the hospital. They found a large amount of money on him, took it, and his clothes. He was not getting out until a legal guardian came to check him out.

It was a good thing that I had POA. My sister and I flew out there immediately.

They had run tests on him and told us he could no longer live alone. I still didn't believe that yet, but they refused to let me take him out until I agreed to their stipulations. They took his driver's license and set up house visits. We drove him home and, after discussing it, decided that he would come home to Minnesota with us and we would have him tested for dementia. He was at my home for five weeks, so my sister who had lived with me for seven years stayed at her daughter's. There were three days of testing, and the results came back four weeks later. He had vascular dementia, and I was told I could no longer let him live alone. It was a struggle to decide what to do.

He was in denial and very independent. In the end, the decision was made by us all—we would let him live in Wyoming while the weather was good, but in the winter, he would come back to Minnesota with us. He agreed. He agreed for us to look for a house he would buy. I learned the hard way that he was not a man of his word and had little care for the expense of the money we would spend to take care of him. I learned some things that I wish that I had not—he was still that father I had pursued all those years. He had not learned with age to value what is valuable. Life was all about him.

James 1:2–3 (NASB) reads, "Count it all joy when you meet trials of many kinds, for you know that the testing of your faith produces endurance."

Romans 5:3–5 (ESV) reads:

> We rejoice in our sufferings, knowing that suffering produces endurance, and endurance produces character, and character produces hope, and hope does not put us to shame, because God's love has been poured into our hearts.

If I had known at the time, I would have never chosen the fork in the road that I took. It would cost me things that I treasured. It would cost me my sister and father. It was a high price to pay.

On the other hand, it was for my sister's ultimate good. She ended up with a home—a good home and the time she needed with my father.

I lost in the things that were visible and tangible, but I gained in the unseen and eternal. I found a pearl of great price—true healing, joy, and peace, though it took some digging to find them. I found an overwhelming portion of God's great love—a double portion. He poured his Father's love into my heart until my cup ran over. I wouldn't trade these light afflictions for anything this world has to offer. It would be like Esau, selling his birthright for a bowl of soup—it was good that I didn't know.

The decision I made that day was to use my 401(k) as proof of our ability to buy the house on Feldman Avenue. It would have never gone through without it.

I have no regrets today. It was a God thing—just a painful thing. There are things we must learn—there are hidden treasures we need to mine. I have no need to rummage through the wreckage, but those four years were full of tears and heartfelt disappointment. God slowly and gently pried my fingers off of my sister and father. I didn't do it willingly, but God was determined for me to let go. When we empty our hands, he fills them with things we really need. He can't fill our hands when they are full of idols—when our eyes are fixed on things other than him.

That was the moment in time when he told me I must stop begging people to love me. It was something I had practiced and picked up from my mother. God taught me that love is always something freely given. Love doesn't look for evil. Love doesn't choose to believe lies. A loving father doesn't use one child to divide a family. Love isn't one-sided. Love is not self-centered.

It is not an easy thing to face the truth that people you thought loved you really don't. They certainly don't stop loving you so easily. There were seeds in the soil that were eager to begin growing. Betrayal is a deep wound—only God's healing goes that deep. It is his finger that must touch the wound.

I eventually got the prayer I needed to break those soul ties, and to my surprise, I was also freed from the soul tie of my second marriage. It was a twofold freedom I had never experienced before.

When chains have bound your heart for so long and they fall to the ground, the freedom is spectacular. I am sure that my sister had some precious moments with my dad, but he was difficult, self-centered, and judgmental. She had her hands full, to say the least.

She told me this story: A very good thing happened on a trip to Wyoming with him. They stopped at the prison museum in Laramie, and she found him looking at a sign on the wall that read, "*Do you need pardon and forgiveness?*" She asked him if he needed pardon and forgiveness. He said yes. She prayed with him, and he cried. My mom's prayers were answered that day, and God gave my sister a gift.

In January 2017, Dad slipped as he started to go downstairs and landed on the landing. Within a few days, he began to have trouble walking. It progressed very quickly to where he needed to be lifted up to even toilet. He was not a big man, but dead weight is difficult to manage. I was leaving for Arizona on February 12 and had plans to be gone for five weeks. I spent over sixty hours with Dad, so my sister could get things done. She was exhausted as he wouldn't let her sleep. Those were the final hours I would spend with him.

He seemed to enjoy being with me and called me his pretty girl again. I hurt my back, trying to lift him, and would need a chiropractor to fix it in Arizona.

The day we flew to Arizona, my beloved aunt Phyllis passed away. I had talked to her one week before when she was in the hospital. I was shocked at this.

The first week in Arizona, I also had two dreams—in the first one, I came down my stairs at my home in Minnesota one morning, and my dad was sitting in my big leather rocking chair. I called my sister on the phone and said, "Why is Dad here?"

She said, "He is not."

In my dream, he was.

The next night, I had another dream. I was in an all-white bedroom with two beds on either side. Everything was white. My dad was in one of the beds, and I laid down beside him. I looked at the other bed, unsure who was in it.

I knew then my father would die soon. The day Dad died, I was back in Minnesota with my husband in the hospital. My husband passed away one week later. I didn't know that he was in the other bed.

My sister would tell me the story: She was bribing Dad to sleep some with the promise of a cookie when he woke. That morning, she was out of homemade cookies and gave him a Fig Newton, which he ate, then said, "This is not a cookie!"

Then he started an argument and told her that she just wanted him to go to hell. She replied that she certainly did not want him to go to hell and went upstairs. When she came back, he was gone.

These are the things that God did for me after Dad died. The first was that he said to me, "Are you done yet?"

It might not sound kind, but it was. He meant, are you done chasing after your father's heart to love you? There was a heavy burden lifted off my shoulders that day. I was ready to let God be the only Father I would seek love from. He is the best Father!

The next thing that happened to me was this—I started to struggle with thoughts of, *Now, I have to live the rest of my life knowing that my dad had tried to disinherit me.* My oldest son tried to console me that it was just his dementia. Many people tried to tell me that. But I had learned that it was much better to face the truth than believe a lie. I went for a walk and wrestled with these thoughts. I am sure some might not believe this, but all of a sudden, I heard my dad deep in my spirit. He told me how sorry he was for hurting me all those years. In heaven, he knew the truth of it all and wanted me to forgive him. I might have thought that I imagined all of this, except that the deep sadness instantly disappeared. I forgave him.

My next experience was from the property in Wyoming. After my dad had up and moved away from the property in Wisconsin and I had driven to Englewood, Colorado, more than once to find that he wasn't there, after that, I refused to go visit him. He moved his wife out to the property in Wyoming.

My brother and his son took a motorcycle trip out there to visit my dad. My brother told me horror stories about Dad's only toilet being in the front yard, out in the open field. I would later learn that this open toilet had been an anniversary gift to my stepmother. And I would later learn that Dad kept asking, "When is Linda going to come out here?"

Apparently, he wanted me to come, but I refused to go until he got a toilet that wasn't in the field.

Then in the summer of 2005, my aunt Phyllis bought a small motor home and came to Wisconsin to pick it up. She was going to drive it back to Arizona. She cautiously asked me if I would like to ride with her to go visit my dad. I agreed, and we had a wonderful trip together. I loved my aunt Phyllis, and she loved my dad.

Everyone was aware of the problem my dad had with his kids. It was not hidden. I was angry at my dad for not loving us. I cried. Then I decided that I would try and understand why Dad loved this place. I opened my eyes to the beauty out there and took hundreds of pictures (some are still in frames around my library). I wrote poems and gave them to him. They are lost now, forever.

There was some healing in my heart, and from that time on, I traveled to Wyoming every year to visit them. After four years of going there, I persuaded my sister to come. They would have never reconciled if I had not been persistent.

God tells us to be persistent in prayer. Some things take time.

This land had been my place of reconnecting with my dad. So after he passed away, I had to go back there one more time. I did this in early May of 2019. There was eight inches of snow on the ground. It was a brave thing to do to—drive down his 3.5-mile driveway full of deep ruts and rocks, all hidden by the snow. But I needed to say goodbye.

I still had not cried about my dad. and I thought that this would be the place. We walked the last half mile, not wanting the car to get stuck out there. His shooting window was opened, and I could have gone in—but I didn't.

There was a surreal peace and quiet in my heart. My times and memories of going there had come to an end. I felt no grief—I thought I would. I only felt loved by my heavenly Father, and that was all I needed.

I never cried one tear when Dad died——not one. I had cried gallons the years before. There were none left.

Down in Florida in January 2020, one morning in church after worship, the pastor got up and said, "This morning, God wants to heal father wounds."

I had forgiven my dad and felt peaceful, but I didn't know that there were still deep places in my heart God knew I needed healing in. I instantly started weeping tears. They ran down my face.

Two mornings later, I woke up early for some reason and started remembering the different times in my life with my dad that left wounds. Much to my surprise, the painful memories were no longer painful.

God doesn't just want us to forgive. He came to heal the brokenhearted.

Second Corinthians 1:3 tells us that he is "the Father of mercies and God of all comfort, who comforts us in all our tribulations, that we may be able to comfort them which are in any trouble" (HCSB).

May your hearts find the comfort and healing that you need.

Chapter 20

Psalm 10:14c (HCSB) reads, "You are the helper of the fatherless."

You do not need to have your father die to be fatherless. There are things worse than your father dying.

I am going back now to the time when I walked through my second divorce because there is a story I must tell. Larry, my third husband, was a longtime postmaster and would eventually retire after thirty-nine years of throwing his whole life into the post office. He was meticulous in details and had the most beautiful printing I had ever seen in a man (usually, you can't read their handwriting). He arrived at our office in October 2003. He was very nervous, easily excitable, and addicted to cigarettes, diet coke, and hostess cupcakes. He was fatherless.

His father had died in his early sixties but had physically and verbally beat him throughout his youth, which deeply damaged who Larry was inside. He self-medicated with his addictions. His pain caused anger and insecurities. He had many fears, and one of them was of being alone.

I had just spent the first year of my life being alone. He was eager to jump in and help me. As I have told in past chapters, he mowed my lawn (which he loved to do) and, eventually moved into the house in Rockford to help me out with the two houses. When the judge kicked me out of the marital house, I had no choice but to move in with him. We also did our Mexico trip in which he crashed the moped and broke bones. I was a stressful time.

In July of 2005, when the divorce was finalized, he wanted to marry right away. I said no. I didn't know what to do. By the next summer, I knew that I needed to decide—marry him or ask him to leave. I chose to love and marry him. Love is always a choice we make.

We married on August 25, 2006. I knew he would never be unfaithful, and God asked me to love him. I did. God loves the fatherless in a special way, and he loves the broken. His heart is to rescue them. He did that for Larry.

God and I held his hand as he walked through the next ten years. It was not always an easy road, and I learned to forgive on nearly a daily basis. He learned to forgive his father and himself. He learned that God loved him, and he accepted God's gift of salvation. If I had not married him, that might not have ever happened. God did this, not me. God's ways are perfect.

It was Memorial weekend of 2016, and I had gone by myself to Wisconsin to be with my aunt and uncle. They were having daily aids come out to help because of Lou's worsening condition with her Parkinson's disease. She had this disease for about seventeen years. Uncle Gene had emphysema and was on oxygen.

I was traveling there four times a year at this point. Lou needed help with almost everything at this stage. The aids were used to me coming, and that holiday weekend, something happened, and they didn't show up. It was uncle Gene and me that weekend.

I had a dream that morning. I dreamed that I was standing on the beach of the ocean. Behind me was a wall made of rocks. As I was standing there, a huge wave came, hitting me and knocking me into the wall. I picked myself up as a second small wave rolled in. Then a second huge wave came and knocked me over again into the wall. This happened three times; after which, I heard a voice calling out my name, "Linda!"

I woke up and realized that Aunt Lou was calling me. It was four-thirty in the morning, and I jumped up to go to her. She was awake and wanted me to be awake with her.

I sat with her for an hour, getting her coffee and holding her hand. Then she dozed back off. I figured that I better get some more sleep if I was going to be taking care of her the rest of the day. I went back to my bedroom, and before I could lie down, God began to speak to me about the dream I had.

This was what he said—I wrote it down: "This is how I will deliver you from the storms of life that will come. It will be like one who wakes up from a dream. The shifts and changes will have no more power over you than that of a dream. I will deliver you in a moment. I will call your name, and the waves will cease. My Presence will be your reality."

When God speaks, you know it, and he speaks with a purpose. My heart was excited at this new experience. God meant something, even though I had no idea what he meant.

That fall, Larry started saying things like, "If I die, make sure you give my girls the things in my storage cases in the garage." Larry was pretty negative, so I said that I didn't really want to talk about him dying—that I wouldn't want to know too much before it happened. He agreed that he didn't want to know either. That was the end of our conversations about death. It turned out we knew less than four weeks before he died.

So we traveled to Arizona on January 12, 2017 for a five-week stay at Sedona. My sister-in-law Lynda came to stay for the first week. We always have such great fun together. I love her. Larry wasn't feeling well and didn't mind staying back at the condo we were in. My aunt had died, and I had, had those two dreams about my dad. There was something in the air.

After Lynda left to go back to Washington, it was clear that Larry needed some attention. So I called around to find a good chiropractor to get his back adjusted. We went in, and he told the chiropractor that his pain level was an eleven.

They did X-rays of his back. The man pulled me aside and told me he could not touch Larry's back because he had lesions between two of his vertebrae. He suggested I take him to the ER. We went and spent the rest of the day there. The doctors came back with the same diagnose and gave him sixteen pain pills. Well, we were going to be there for almost four more weeks—that would never last.

The next day I drove him up to Flagstaff to see a specialist. They set us up for MRIs in Cottonwood a few days later and gave us enough pain pills to give him four pills a day until we went back home. The day we went in for the MRI, he was getting worse and having trouble breathing. After the MRI, I brought him to the Cottonwood ER where he spent the rest of the day. They released him with an oxygen tank.

A few days later, I brought him back, and they admitted him into the hospital. I watched as they put a tube into his lung and drained one and a half quarts of dark-brown liquid from his lung. When I came back the next morning to be with him, he told me about something he had experienced the night before.

He said that after the nurses had left and it was semi-dark in the room, he looked at the window and had a vision. He said that he saw what looked like our pastor, playing the piano, and three of his friends, standing and worshipping God. He listed them in this order—John, Eric, and Gary. When they finished singing, they turned and looked at him. At that point, he realized that it was not our pastor but, rather, the pastor's father, playing the piano.

I asked Larry what he thought all of that meant. His response was, "They have my back!"

I said nothing to Larry about what I thought. He was happy.

To finish this part of the story, Larry is buried directly in front of his three friends, who had passed away before him. They are in that exact order—John, Eric, and Gary. Our pastor's father is over to the side. Larry didn't know these things.

He later thanked me for not telling him at that point—that I knew then that he was going home shortly to be with Jesus. Larry spent most of those four weeks in the hospital or in doctor's offices. His lung was drained again. The fluids were building up.

It was a nightmare getting Larry back home to Minnesota, but in all of our troubles, God was always there to help us. We made it home.

The next day, I took him to our doctor, who gave us the sad news that Larry should go home and prepare to die. It was a sobering day for him. I had to take him to the hospital again that night. Our pastor and his wife helped me. He spent six more days there. They were good days for Larry and me. We had good conversations, and his inhibitions were gone. It was a sweet time I will cherish.

It was at that point that my father died. I was later to learn that my uncle Ralph left this world around this same time too. I loved Uncle Ralph and Aunt Phyllis.

That was four—with Aunt Lou passing in June that year, and Uncle Gene leaving one year after my father. That makes six.

But back to Larry—that week, he said things like, "God told me I would go easily," "God told me he would be there to meet me," "How will I find you, Linda?", "I want you to marry, again," "I am so sorry that I wasn't a good husband to you."

Now that was not like Larry—none of it. We set up hospice and brought him home. He stayed with us only two and a half days from that point. He left well, and I am so proud of him.

The evening before he went home to be with Jesus, all of the kids came over, except Larry's youngest daughter, to say goodbye. (Mark was deployed.) It was precious. Peyton brought a picture she had painted.

There were many tears, and my little Noah watched earnestly and did what his heart told him to. He is just a little sweetheart. He watched and passed out Kleenexes to wipe away the tears. Some told Larry they were sorry—then Larry wanted to sit up, and this was what he said, "I want you to know that I loved you more than I ever knew how to show you. I am sorry."

He called Emmy to his side and told her to be a good girl—that he would be watching.

There were more tears. I hear that this is not normal for someone a few hours before they die—especially someone on morphine. He didn't want to leave me, but he did early the next morning. His memorial service packed the church, and my best friend said that it was the most beautiful service she had ever attended.

It was—

I have since felt Larry's presence, and he had more joy that day than words could ever say. It was a hard ten years, but it ended well, and his hard work will take care of me for the rest of my days. I will always be grateful.

Right after he died, Peyton said he visited her. My granddaughter Maleia also told me that he came to her in a dream during a very difficult time for her and told her that he always loved her. She said she won't forget that. Larry also told me to give his car to Brandon because he was sorry for the way he had been so unloving to him. I did.

My prophetic dream and the presence of the Lord carried me through those days of loss. It was a dream and promise that will carry me for the rest of my days here on this earth. Words could never express the depth of my thankfulness to the Lord.

Chapter 21

First John 4:20b (ESV) reads, "For he who does not love his brother whom he has seen, cannot love God whom he has not seen."

God never makes mistakes—not even when he creates families. My siblings are my brother and sister because he chose us to be siblings. There was a reason. I know that my brother and sister have their own stories. They will have to tell them themselves. I will tell my story from the one side of the wall they have erected around their lives.

I know this—God loves them, and God loves me. He loves us.

I believe with all my heart that my brother's intentions were genuine—to be a better father to his children than my father was to him. We look at our parents and see things that hurt our hearts, and we are determined to do better with our children.

You can always tell what a person loves in this world. It will be what they spend their time doing and what they spend their money on. It is a dead giveaway, a litmus test—tried and true. My father loved money and himself.

My brother never had trouble spending his money on his family, but it was a hard thing for him to handle. In the beginning, I believe that he meant well. But he failed to give them the thing my father never gave him—genuine love, affection, and acceptance. Money without genuine love will not produce the good desired fruit in the end. The fruit is always revealed in the end.

Children need to know that their parents see value in them. That needs to come from more than their mothers. To not value your children is to not value yourself. Our children came from us and are part of us, but one can never really love others until you first love yourself. Love must always start in the right place, and my brother never learned to truly love himself. There were years of depression, mistakes, and disappointments. Bitterness is an evil poison that effects all you touch. It is easy to do, but we are warned by God to avoid its destructive and deceptive path. One should always listen to what God says. He means what he says.

My heart wants to make excuses for my brother. Is it my dad's fault for not showing him approval? I can't honestly say. Did all of this happen because of sibling rivalry and jealousy? I can't say. I want to look for a reason. Sometimes, we just don't know. I think, in my own reasoning, that if we knew the source, it could be fixed. I would like that. Is this all my fault? I know the answer to that one—no. We can't help who controlled our childhood, but we are accountable for our adult choices.

False religion will never produce good fruit. It can't. It is not possible.

Sometime around 2001, I sent my brother a letter, expressing the desire for us to get to know each other, as we hadn't throughout the years. The year 2003 was a good year for us. He visited and helped me reproduce pictures of my children. These became beautiful books I put together for each of them and gave them to the kids when they married. I will always be thankful for that gift he gave to me.

I remember sharing a scripture with him from Isaiah 46:3–4 (ESV):

> Listen to me, who have been borne by me from before your birth, carried from the womb; even to your old age I am he, and to gray hairs I will carry you. I have made and I will bear; I will carry and save.

I had never seen my brother cry before. I thought family was important to him, as he traveled about to all the families, copying the photos of everyone. It was amazing. I have the copies of those CDs.

I have always loved my brother's children. They are wonderful human beings. I see that. Mandy, the oldest, was born in Germany. She is an introvert, very quiet, compliant, sweet, and a very good daughter. She loves her mom. I see that. She and her husband have given my brother two beautiful grandsons.

My brother spent twenty years as a drill sergeant in the military. He forgot that his children were not soldiers to train. Katie, his middle child, did not take kindly to his demanding and judgmental practices. She did not respond submissively like her older sister. There were several incidents that happened. I remember two—

He had superglued her radio to the Christian station, and she had a boyfriend he didn't approve of. This landed her in the foster care system. I had always loved her and drove to the state of Washington to bring her back to Minnesota. She did not need what I had needed at fifteen. I needed love. She needed freedom. I had to let her go and, for years, felt that I had failed her.

Today, she is forty-five and the single mother of an eleven-year-old boy. My brother has not spoken to her in over twenty years. I am proud of her. She has made some mistakes but has become a beautiful woman. I want her father wounds to be healed—so does God.

My nephew is a most wonderful man. My brother idolized him until he became an adult and no longer followed my brother's wishes. I couldn't imagine my brother turning on him, but he did. I identified with Bob, as he played the role of peacemaker in the family. I am acquainted with that role.

My father had four wonderful grandsons that he never gave one moment of his heart too. He was blind to all that he threw away—his granddaughters and grandsons alike.

My brother became like my father—only my brother also carried bitterness in his bag. I will never understand why. My hope is that he figures it out before it is too late.

As for his children, God has got them—he will always be the Father to the fatherless.

Lynda, his ex-wife is my wonderful friend! She is a very happy, creative, and artsy person. She wakes up early in the morning and looks for adventure and beauty. She loves to travel like me, and we have had some memorable vacations together. She has become my beloved sister. Her heart was deeply wounded by my brother, but she pushes on with courage, strength, and unfailing love for her children and three grandsons. I love her dearly. My prayer for her is that her heart finds healing too.

It is *okay* to cry. God has tender compassion on the brokenhearted. Tears bring healing.

I always dreamed, after my parents were gone, that my brother, sister, and I would vacation together and have many adventures. Sometimes dreams are only that—something you had hoped for.

My sister, on the other hand—we spent many years being close friends after she became a single mother, when her youngest daughter was very small. We did trips together, which brought me great joy.

The first trip was even with my brother out West, where we white-water rafted in Idaho. We also did a trip to West Virginia and rafted on the New River. The final trip was to take my dad out to the Grand Tetons. These are memories that I cherish. My heart was open to my little sister and my home too, where she lived for seven years. We walked together as she finished her years of study to become a massage therapist of which she is excellent at. I love my sister.

My mother wrote a poem to us back in those painful years. This is what she wrote:

> To my darling little daughters,
> As you travel down life's road,
> May your eyes be always lifted,
> To the master of your soul.
>
> When life's temptations greet you,
> And the tempter's voice you hear,
> May this knowledge be your comfort
> That your savior's ever near.
>
> Let the Holy Spirit guide you,
> In decisions great and small,
> Seek his help what-e're you do,
> And he will always hear your call.

My sister chose a fork in the road some ten years ago. I haven't seen my sister/friend since. Once in a while, there has been a faint glimpse of her shadow, but it disappears as silently as it had appeared—and it is gone.

She lives only 3.5 miles away from me, and I find it interesting—that is the same length of Dad's driveway in Wyoming. I have stopped staring out the window for her, but I do watch now and then. But I am still waiting—

It is hard to turn around on a path you have chosen to travel, but it is never too late. Stubbornness makes some things hard to do. It is through faith and patience that we inherit God's promises. Coming home might seem impossible sometimes, but I have found that if we choose to put our foot down, God will create a way that didn't exist before we placed our foot there. He will make a way where there was none. He creates new paths for our wounded hearts. He is good at taking the hardness out of our hearts. He will give us a new, tender heart.

If you have found yourself far from where you have wanted to be, there is a way back to the one who really loves you. God made a way through his son, Jesus. He is the way, the truth, and the life.

When we acknowledge that we have made a wrong choice, we can come home. We can pray—God listens to our hearts when we cry out to him.

> *Father, I am sorry for my sin. I am lost and need you to save me.*
> *I acknowledge that you are God, and I give my heart to you.*
> *Forgive me for my sins and wash my heart clean.*
> *I put my trust in you alone and surrender my life.*
> *In Jesus's name. Amen.*

If you have never given your heart to him—I encourage you to do so. If you have wandered away because of pain or sin or unbelief, turn around and come home. The Father is calling your name and watching for you.

Life is a vapor in the wind. It is like the grass of the fields and its flowers. The wind passes over them, and they are gone. Eternity is forever.

Chapter 22

There is a rather large plaque on the wall in my library. It has been there for many years. When I saw it at the store, I knew that it belonged to me because it had been written on my heart—all of my life. It was a reflection of something that I knew to be true.

It reads like this: "*Let us be silent that we may hear the whisper of God.*"

This has been true since eternity.

More than 10,000 years ago, it is recorded in the Bible (1 Kings 19) that the prophet Elijah found that God was not in the strong wind or the earthquake or the fire, but he was in the still, small voice. Elijah had run away in fear from a wicked queen—he was hiding, and he was feeling sorry for himself to the point that he asked God to end his life.

I have been there. I have been there when the winds were too strong for me and my world was shaking and fire was consuming much of my life. I didn't want to remain either, but then I heard a still, small voice calling out to me—I heard it in the middle of the winds. I called it a hurricane back in those days.

It can be hard to be quiet in this noisy world. There is noise everywhere. It is external and internal. There are the voices of others, replaying over and over in our heads. It is hard to stop them. Something said once can wound us a thousand times—echoing and echoing. This will continue as long as you allow it to. It will continue until you let God help you.

There is wisdom in silence if you turn your heart to the source of truth. You can hear the whisper of God—go out into nature. Choose to be alone. Turn the volume of the world off and sit and wait. Bring your Bible. Check out Ephesians chapter 2 (NASB). It reads:

> And you were dead in the trespasses and sins in which you once walked, following the course of this world. We all once lived in the passions of our flesh, carrying out the desires of the body and the mind. *But God*—being rich in mercy, because of the great love with which He loved us. Made us alive together with Christ. So that in the ages to come he might show the immeasurable riches of his grace in kindness toward us in Christ Jesus.

I don't want to be so deaf that I cannot hear the voice of God. I listened far too long to the voices of others, who couldn't even see me, no less tell me the truth.

I was told over and over by my second husband that I wanted things that I was never going to have. That was a lie. My heart told me that I was created to be truly loved—deeply and faithfully loved. I thought that was just a fairy tale—too good to be true. That was a lie.

One day, God told me that he was the one who put that desire into my heart. I didn't understand it because I had tried so hard to make it come true and failed. Our efforts always fail. God is not a tease. He is after our hearts. He is pursuing us and wants us to stop and listen.

After my Dad, Larry, and my aunt and uncle died, I understood the dream I had, had back on Memorial Day 2016. I should have been devastated, but God's presence carried me over much of the grief. I am grateful for them in my life, but they were not the source of my joy.

Instead of holding tightly to the loss, I chose joy. I had not lost the one who truly loved me. He was still there, carrying me over all of it. He filled my heart with songs of praise and peace. Death has no power over you when you know the resurrection and the life.

I had people accuse me of just not loving them—that couldn't be farther than the truth. I carried the prince of peace within me, and he brings peace that the world cannot understand.

Two months after my husband died, I heard God whisper to my heart, "You are not going to spend the rest of your life alone."

Well, now I was on a first-name basis with him, and I laughed. Seriously, I have to do this again? Really? There was silence from him. So I figured I would argue a little—I did.

The silence continued, so I thought I would be smart and try a different approach. I gave him a list of four things that I would have to see before I ever looked at a man again. I thought that I had won the argument—the last of the four was, "He would have to see me through God's eyes and love me through God's heart."

I was a little smug, as that was not in the realm of possibilities in my understanding. I didn't know that there was a man who had been praying for two years for a godly wife. I didn't know that there was a man who, out of his severe rebellion, had been broken by the kindness of God—a man who, too, was listening to the whisper of God, who had been looking for someone who could see him through God's eyes and love him through God's heart.

There has been so much in my life that I didn't know, but I know the one who knows everything—before the foundation of the world, he knew me and called me by name.

While I was in my mother's womb, there was a book written with all of my days ordained in it (Psalm 139 NASB). He knew every sin and rebellious way I would choose, and he stepped in and paid the debt that I owed. He suffered unspeakable pain so that I could find healing for my wounds. He is the very best Father and decided to give me something that I had not even dared to ask for anymore. It was a gift no one but him could ever give me.

The week that my aunt Lou passed into eternity, Warren stepped into my life. I will spare you all the details which I have told over and over.

We began having dinner together in July 2017 on Monday nights. We sat at the table and talked and talked and talked. We talked about God. We talked about our failures and wrong choices. He was listening. So was I.

I personally had never experienced a man open enough and fearless enough to admit their weaknesses and failures. He came from an entirely different planet and world than I had, yet we ended up at the exact same place and time.

This is something that only God could do. It was a tremendous miracle to me. He was a perfect gentleman all those months and did not even try to kiss me. For the first time in my life, I felt perfectly safe and protected. I looked up the meaning of his name—it means, "protecting friend."

Names mean important things. They are not random, not when you belong to God. They call into being things that do not exist. God sees us before we become. When we surrender our lives to him and believe—we become his children, and we are loved by the very best Father. I am and always will be a daddy's girl.

Warren and I were married on April 28, 2018. In my heart, it will go down as a day of blessing beyond my wildest dreams. I dream wildly.

I am that little girl who danced though the fields with wonder, looking for adventure, listening—listening for the voice of the one who created me and called me to take hold of his hand and walk through this world, telling those around me that there is good news.

In my years of delivering mail, I knew that I was called to bring news—good news. There is hope. There is the one who came to rescue us. There is Jesus.

I have no idea what tomorrow will bring. Warren has asked God to give us another twenty years together. He wants to do wild adventures here before we go. We will see.

My heart has room for more adventures, even though I am deeply satisfied with the goodness of God and his great kindness to me. My deep longing is that you, too, will discover his loving-kindness to you as well.

That is my purpose for this writing—

Chapter 23

Romans 5:10 (RSV) reads, "For if while we were enemies we were reconciled to God by the death of his Son, much more now that we are reconciled, shall we be saved by his life."

His love was, is greater than my sin.

More than twenty years ago, a friend of mine, Linda Alexander, gave me a book. The name of the book was *the Sacred Romance* by Brent Curtis and John Eldredge.

As the title represents, it is the story of how God passionately pursues us in his great love—all of our lives. This book was the awakening to me that, someday, I would be writing my story of God's reckless and unrelenting pursue of my heart. I fully identified with his declaration that, within our hearts, God has put the need for three things: beauty, adventure, and romance.

There were two more books that followed in John Eldredge's writings called *Wild at Heart* and *the Journey of Desire*. In the book *Journey of Desire*, he told a short story that I would like to share with you. I have been granted the permission to share it in this book. It is about a sea lion.

I was that sea lion. Maybe you are too. Listen with your heart.

> Once upon a time there lived a sea lion who had lost the sea.
>
> He lived in a country known as the barren lands. High on a plateau, far from any coast, it was a place so dry and dusty that it could only be called a desert. A kind of coarse grass grew

in patches here and there, and a few trees were scattered across the horizon. But mostly, it was dust. And sometimes wind, which together make one very thirsty. Of course, it must seem strange to you that such a beautiful creature should wind up in a desert at all. He was, mind you, a sea lion. But things like this do happen.

How the sea lion came to the barren lands, no one could remember.

It all seemed so long ago. So long, in fact, it appeared as though he had always been there. Not that he belonged in such an arid place.

How could that be? He was, after all, a sea lion. But as you know, once you have lived so long in a certain spot, no matter how odd, you come to think of it as home.

There was a time, many years back, when the sea lion knew he was lost.

In those days, he would stop every traveler he met to see if he might help him find his way back to the sea. But no one seemed to know the way.

On he searched, but never finding. After years without success, the sea lion took refuge beneath a solitary tree, beside a very small water hole. The tree provided refuge from the burning rays of the sun, which was very fierce in that place. And the water hole, though small and muddy, was wet, in its own way. Here he settled down and got on the as best he could.

Had you journeyed in those days through the barren lands, you might have seen the sea lion for yourself. Quite often in the evening, he would go and sit upon his favorite rock, a very large boulder, which lifted him off the burning sand and allowed him a view of the entire country.

There he would remain for hours into the night, silhouetted against the sky. And on the best nights, when the wind shifted to the east, a faint smell of salt air would come to him on the breeze. Then he would close his eyes and imagine himself once more at the sea. When he lay himself down to sleep, he would dream of a vast, deep ocean. Twisting and turning, diving and twirling, he would swim and swim and swim. When he woke, he thought he heard the sound of breakers. The sea was calling to him.

The sea lion loved his rock, and he even loved waiting night after night for the sea breezes that might come. Especially he loved the dreams those memories would stir. But as you well know, even the best of dreams cannot go on, and in the morning when the sea lion woke, he was still in the barren lands. Sometimes he would close his eyes and try to fall back asleep.

It never seemed to work, for the sun was always bright.

Eventually, it became too much for him to bear. He began to visit his rock only on occasion. "I have too much to do," he told himself. "I cannot waste my time just idling about." He really did not have so much to do. The truth of it was, waking so far from home was such a disappointment, he did not want to have those wonderful dreams anymore. The day finally came when he stopped going to his rock altogether, and he no longer lifted his nose to the wind when the sea breezes blew.

The sea lion was not entirely alone in those parts. For it was there he met the tortoise. Now this tortoise was an ancient creature, so weathered by his life in the barren lands that at first, the sea lion mistook him for a rock.

He told the tortoise of his plight, hoping that this wise one might be able to help him. "Perhaps," the tortoise mused, "this is the sea." His eyes appeared to be shut against the bright sun, but he was watching the sea lion very closely. The sea lion swept his flippers once against his side, gliding to the end of the water hole and back. "I don't know," he said. It isn't very deep." "Isn't it?" "Somehow, I thought that the sea would be broader, deeper. At least, I hoped so." "You must learn to be happy here," the tortoise told him one day.

"For it is unlikely you shall ever find this sea of yours." Deep in his old and shriveled heart, the tortoise envied the sea lion and his sea. "But I belong to the sea. We are made for each other." "Perhaps. But you have been gone so long now, the sea has probably forgotten you." This thought had never occurred to the sea lion. But it was true, he had been gone for a long, long time.

"If this is not my home, how can I ever feel at home here?" the sea lion asked.

"You will, in time." The tortoise appeared to be squinting, his eyes a thin slit.

"I have seen the sea, and it is no better than what you have found here." "You have seen the sea!" "Yes, Come closer," whispered the tortoise, "and I will tell you a secret. I am not a tortoise. I am a sea turtle. But I left the sea of my own accord, many years ago, in search of better things.

If you stay with me, I will tell you stories of my adventures." The stories of the ancient tortoise were enchanting and soon cast their spell upon the sea lion. As weeks passed into months, his memory of the sea faded. "The desert," whispered the tortoise, "is all that is, or was, or ever will be." When the sun grew fierce and burned his skin, the sea lion would hide in the shade of the tree, listening to the tales woven by the tortoise. When the dry winds cracked his flippers and filled his eyes with dust, the sea lion would retreat to the water hole. And so the sea lion remained, living his days between water hole and tree. The sea no longer filled his dreams.

It was in May that the winds began to blow. The sea lion had grown used to wind, and at first he did not pay much heed at all. Years of desert life had taught him to turn his back in the direction from which the winds came and cover his eyes with his flippers, so that the dust would not get in. Eventually, the winds would always pass.

But not this time. Day and night it came, howling across the barren lands.

There was nothing to stop its fury, nothing to even slow it down. For forty days and forty nights the wind blew. And then, just as suddenly as it had begun, it stopped. The sea lion lifted himself to have a look around.

He could hardly believe his eyes.

Every single leaf had been stripped from his tree. The branches that remained, with only a twig or two upon them, looked like an old scarecrow.

And I do not need to tell you there was no longer shade in which to hide. But worse than this, much worse indeed, was what the sea lion saw next.

The water hole was completely dry.

Three weeks after the wind ceased to blow, the sea lion had a dream. Now, as I told you before, there were other nights in which he had dreamed of the sea.

But those were long ago and nearly forgotten. Even still, the ocean that filled his dreams this night was so beautiful and clear, so vast and deep, it was as if he were seeing it for the very first time. The sunlight glittered on its surface, and as he dived, the waters all around him shone like an emerald. If he swam quite deep it turned to jade, cool and dark and mysterious. But he was never frightened, not at all. For I must tell you that in all his dreams of the sea, he had never found himself in the company of other sea lions. This night there were many, round about him, diving and turning, spinning and twirling. They were playing.

Oh, how he hated to wake up from that wonderful dream. The tears running down his face were the first wet thing he had felt in three weeks. But he did not pause even to wipe them away, he did not pause, in fact, for anything at all.

He set his face to the east, and began to walk as best a sea lion can.

"Where are you going?" asked the tortoise.

"I am going to find the sea."

*Let the morning bring me word of your unfailing
love, for I have put my trust in you.
Show me the way I should go, for to you I entrust my life.
Rescue me from my enemies, Lord, for I hide myself in you.
Teach me to do your will, for you are my God;
May your good spirit lead me on level ground.
For your name's sake, Lord preserve my life;
in your righteousness, bring me out of trouble.
In your unfailing love, silence my enemies.*

—Psalm 143:8–12 (NIV)

MY FAMILY

Michelle Christine

The language/cultural origin of this name is Hebrew from the name *Michal.*

The inherent meaning is "who is like God?"

The spiritual meaning is "godliness."

The inherent meaning of *Christine* is "follower of Christ" and "true disciple."

When my daughter was a little girl, a friend spoke a prophetic word over her—her life would open up like a beautiful rose, and the fragrance would spill forth.

True beauty, sometimes, comes out of ashes, and fragrance comes from first being crushed. God always looks at the heart and not as man sees on the outward appearance. The opinions of the world are of little value and have no lasting effect. We, as human beings, are desirous of being seen outwardly, but God is desirous of the beauty that comes only from what is formed within.

His ways are not our ways, and his thoughts are not our thoughts. God sees her. He has called her to be a beautiful fragrance. He called her into being while still in my womb. God is faithful to all he promises.

She has always been very motivated in her life. She is full of creativity, intelligence, perseverance, adventure, and independence. She traveled as a young adult, alone to Northern Ireland for her last two years of college. It was an adventure she had dreamed of from a young girl. It formed strength in her.

The scriptural promise God has given to me for my daughter is from Hosea 2 (ESV). It is my heart's prayer for her.

> Therefore, I will hedge up her way with thorns, and I will build a wall against her, so that she cannot find her paths. I will allure her and bring her into the wilderness and speak tenderly to her. And there I will give her her vineyards and make the Valley of Achor a door of hope—and say to her, I will make you lie down in safety. And I will betroth you to me forever. I will betroth you to me in righteousness and in justice, in steadfast love and in mercy. I will betroth you to me in faithfulness. And you shall know the Lord.

Isaiah 62:11–12 (HCSB) reads:

> Say to daughter Zion; Behold, your salvation is coming. Behold, His reward is with Him, and His gifts accompany Him, and they will be called the Holy People, the Lord's redeemed; and you will be called Cared For, a City not Deserted.

Isaiah 63:9 (KJV) reads:

> In all their affliction He was afflicted and the Angel of His presence saved them. In His love and in His pity he redeemed them; and He bare them, and carried them all the days of old.

Brandon Michael

The language/cultural origin of this name is either Old Irish or Old English.

If coming from the Irish, it means "prince" or "brave."

If from the English, it means "beacon hill" or "lighthouse." A beacon is a guide or a source of inspiration.

An old plaque I found said this about the name:

> He is an interesting conversationalist
> Brandon has a heart for helping others
> Confident when faced with adversity
> His family's welfare is his primary concern
> He is admired for his unwavering loyalty
> His words are full of wisdom and insight

The spiritual meaning is "fervent," "having or displaying a passionate intensity."

When he was a very young child, he had great determination and intensity. Holding him down was no small task. With great humor, I remember a three-hour battle to get him to eat two green beans—and I am not sure if I won that battle.

He mellowed considerably as he grew and became much more contemplative as the world opened up before him. He is moving forward with his life with determination, maturity, and tenacity.

I have a plaque I purchased many years ago in Hawaii—

DETERMINATION: with tenacity, one flourishes in the face of adversity.

The scriptures for Brandon are from Luke 1:77–79, Psalm 27:1, John 8:12 (ESV).

> To give knowledge of salvation to his people in the forgiveness of their sins, because of the tender mercy of our God—
> To give Light to those who sit in darkness and the shadow of death, To guide our feet into the way of Peace.
> The Lord is my light and my salvation; whom shall I fear?
> The Lord is the stronghold of my life; of who shall I be afraid?
> Then Jesus spoke to them again: "I am the light of the world. Whoever follows Me will not walk in darkness, but will have the light of life."

God is the defender and father of the fatherless—

Maleia Julia

The language/cultural origin of this is a Christian Hawaiian name.

The inherent meaning is "calm" or "gentle waters," and in another searching, I found its meaning to be "beloved."

The spiritual connotation is "forgiven."

The name *Julia* means "youthful" and "guided by faith."

She came into the world crying. I couldn't even console her for a short period. She was reacting to the pain her mama was experiencing. She has never liked conflict from the moment she entered the world. Her heart wants peace, and there is an internal reaction that rises up when there are any signs to the contrary. She would defend her brother with urgency if I even raised my voice to him. I understand, as I have wrestled with those issues—there is part of me inside her heart. Fear can seem like a giant to a little girl. That is why Jesus came to be the prince of peace to our hearts.

There is conflict in this world that is far too big for a little girl to carry. She shouldn't.

My favorite things that she said when she was small are:

There was a tornado warning when she was about four, and they came over to my home.

She rushed into my arms, saying, "Grandma, Grandma, there are tomatoes coming in the sky!"

At another time, as we were snuggled on the couch, she said, "I love this couch!" and I asked her why. Her response was, "Because every time I sit here with you, I am loved."

There are memories to cherish—

The scriptures for her are from Romans 8:1, 18, 28–30 (ESV):

> There is therefore now no condemnation for those who are in Christ Jesus—for I consider that the sufferings of this present time are not worth comparing to the glory that is to be revealed to us.
>
> And we know that for those who love God all things work together for good, for those who are called according to his purpose. For those whom he foreknew he also predestined to be conformed to the image of his Son—and those he predestined he also called, and those whom he called he also justified, and those whom he justified he also glorified.
>
> What then shall we say to these things? If God is for us, who can be against us?
>
> He who did not spare his own Son but gave him up for us all, how will he not also with him graciously give us all things? Who can bring any charge against God's elect? It is God who justifies. Who is to condemn? Jesus Christ is the one who died—more than that, who was raised—who is at the right hand of God, who is indeed interceding for us. Who shall separate us from the love of God? Shall tribulation, or distress, or persecution, or famine, or nakedness, or danger, or sword? No, in all these things we are more than conquerors through him who loved us. For I am sure that neither death nor life, not angels nor rulers, nor things present nor things to come, nor powers, nor height nor depth nor anything else in all of creation, will be able to separate us from the love of God in Christ Jesus our Lord.

Michael Frederick

The language/cultural origin of this name is Hebrew.

The inherent meaning is "who is like God?" and the spiritual connotation is "esteemed."

The term *Who is like God?* really means "Who could possibly be as great as God?"

The name *Michael* is mentioned five times in the Bible and referred to the chief prince, an angel who wars in the heavenlies.

Angels are sent by God to serve those who are to inherit salvation. Psalm 91 tells us that "God will command his angels concerning you, to guard you in all your ways."

The name *Frederick* means "peaceful ruler" and the spiritual connotation is "perceptive."

Michael grew very fast from his birth but didn't start to talk until he was two, and then he didn't stop. He was fun-loving and got hurt often in his adventures. He was very protective of his sister, as they were close growing up.

One time, she stirred up a wasp nest on the open front porch, and when he heard her crying, he came running around the house at the same time I carried her around the other side. I found him covered with wasps. I pulled them out of his mouth and off him everywhere, then carried him away as well. We took a trip to the emergency room at the hospital that day as he began to swell from the stings. He was two and a half.

Though all the kids loved their Mom, he was always my defender. I didn't know it until later, but he did torment his youngest brother. He got into the most mischief in his teenage years.

One day, he came to me and said, "Mom, I am going to do some things that you are not going to like, but I want you to know that when I am older, I am going to be just like you and believe in God."

He would have to tell his own story. That was what happened—and God captured his heart.

The scriptures for him are Deuteronomy 31:6, Isaiah 51:16, Isaiah 54:10, 13–17 (ESV).

> Be strong and courageous. Do not fear or be in dread of them, for it is the Lord your God who goes with you. He will not leave you or forsake you.
>
> I have put My words in your mouth, and covered you in the shadow of My hand.
>
> My love will not be removed from you and My covenant of peace will not be shaken. Then all your children will be taught of the Lord, and great will be their peace and you will be established on a foundation of righteousness—if anyone attacks you, it is not from Me; whoever attacks you will fall before you. No weapon formed against you will succeed, and you will refute any accusation. This is the heritage of the Lord's servants and their righteousness is from Me.

Heidi Debra

The language/cultural origin is old German.

The inherent meaning is "noble one" or "nobility," "of noble birth."

To be noble is to be honest and charitable.

The spiritual meaning is "honored" or "blessed."

Other traits found are kindness, adventurous, and independent.

The inherent meaning of the name *Debra* is "honeybee."

The spiritual connotation is "leadership." In the Bible, she was a prophetess who lead Israel into battle and wrote a victory song.

In the years that I have known her, she has consistently been a helping, caring, and sensitive young woman—eager to see the needs of others and lend a helping hand. Much to my joy, she has heard God call her name—responding willingly and eagerly to take his hand and learn to follow him with joy. Her gratitude has overflowed into prayers for her family, husband, and children. She is a blessing to all who cross her path—me included.

The scriptures for her are Psalm 45:13–15 (CSB), Proverbs 31:10–12, 30–31(HCSB).

> In her chamber, the royal daughter is all glorious, her clothing embroidered with gold. In colorful garments she is lead to the King; after her—her companions are brought to you. They are led in with gladness and rejoicing; they enter the king's palace.
>
> Who can find a capable wife? She is far more precious than jewels.

The heart of her husband trusts her, and he will not lack anything good.

She rewards him with good, not evil, all the days of her life.

Charm is deceptive and beauty is fleeting, but the woman who fears the Lord will be praised. Give her the reward of her labor, and let her works praise her at the city gates.

Owen Michael

The language /cultural origin of Owen is Welch.

The inherent meaning is "noble," "wellborn," and "young warrior."

The spiritual connotation is "pleasant to look upon."

In another place, it lists personality traits such as the ability to persuade others effortlessly, expressive, optimistic, outgoing, charming, and cheerful.

Owen came into this world on the very day of my great uncle Charlie's memorial service on October 30, 2005. I was in Grand Rapids when Michael called. Michael cried with emotion at the birth of his son. I lost my uncle, but God gave me a gift to replace him in my heart. These things have meaning to me, as God knows my love language.

Owen is much like Mike when he was young—fun-loving, full of humor and adventure. As he is still a very young man, I have yet to see him take too much seriously. His humor is contagious. You can't help but smile.

My favorite memory of him as a very young child happened one weekend while he was spending the night. He was upset with me for some reason and wouldn't let me catch him. He could outrun me and thought that was quite humorous. I think it took me fifteen minutes to finally catch him. He was having so much fun. By the time I did catch him, he had forgotten why he was angry. We just hugged and laughed. I was worn out. He has long legs.

The scriptures for him are Psalm 16:3, 5–6, 11a (NASB), Proverbs 4:20–21(HCSB).

> As for the saints that are in the earth, they are the majestic ones, in whom is all my delight. Lord, you are my portion and my cup of blessing; You hold my future. The boundary lines have fallen for me in pleasant places; indeed, I have a beautiful inheritance. You reveal the path of life to me; in Your presence is abundant joy; in Your right hand are pleasures for evermore.
>
> My son, pay attention to my words; listen closely to my sayings. Don't lose sight of them; keep them within your heart. For they are life to those who find them, and health to one's whole body. Guard your heart above all else, for it is the source of life.

Peyton Louise

The language/cultural origin of the name Peyton is English or Scottish.

The inherent meaning is "warrior's estate" or "belongs to warriors."

From the Scottish, it means "royal."

The spiritual connotation is "Christlike."

The meaning of *Louise* is a "watchful protectress."

As a very young girl, she was full of adventure and fearless—you had to keep your eye on her as she was quick to run, and she moved fast. Maybe that was the point at which Mike put a fence around their yard. I don't know!

While having lunch at Lord Fletcher's one time with her parents, I heard the story that she jumped off of the pier to swim with the fish. It caused quite a disturbance.

She loves the water and swims very well. Another time, she decided to run away for some reason, but she wanted to bring two suitcases—one was to bring the quilt I had just given to her for her birthday. I just love her.

As she has grown, she has discovered a love for drawing, which I am sure she has found both pleasure and peace as she works on her artistic skills. She draws cartoons but also pictures of those she loves. She loves passionately and is a good friend. Of all of the granddaughters, she looks the most like me.

The scriptures for her are Proverbs 31:25–26 (HCSB), Zephaniah 3:14–17 (NASB).

> Strength and dignity are her clothing, and she laughs at the time to come.
>
> She opens her mouth with wisdom and the teaching of kindness is on her tongue.
>
> Shout for joy, daughter of Zion! Shout in triumph—rejoice and triumph with all your heart. The Lord has taken away His judgements against you, He has cleared away your enemies. The Lord is in your midst; You will no longer fear disaster. The Lord your God is in your midst, a victorious Warrior. He will rejoice over you with joy!
>
> He will quiet you with His love.
>
> He will rejoice over you with shouts of joy!

Matthew David

The language/cultural origin is Hebrew.

The inherent meaning is "gift of God" and "recompense."

God is the great equalizer, and he steps in and gives what is necessary to balance things out. Matthew was that gift to balance out my pain.

The spiritual connotation is "honor to God"—to honor is to regard and treat with admiration and respect or esteem greatly.

The name David means "beloved," and the spiritual connotation is "lover of all."

I certainly don't know how my children's names came to fit them so well, but again, God knew them long before I met them. He created them.

As I have said in the past, Matthew was a sweetheart. When I was pregnant with Mark, he would pat my stomach and tell me to open my mouth. Then he would say, "I love you, baby!"

It was hard to have conflict with him as he was so easygoing. That did become a problem for him in his teen years as he did not know how to say no to wrong choices. Like his mother, conflict was not something he had experience handling. There were things he needed to learn the hard way.

I didn't know how to teach the kids those kind of things. You can never give something that you don't have yourself. He came into a personal relationship with Jesus after a traumatic experience with crashing his first car.

He doesn't like changes and never enjoyed adjusting to new things, like moving, changing jobs, and he fell in love with his first girlfriend whom he married.

He is peace-loving and will rarely say unkind things. His calmness has led him to the ability to not react to the pressures of momentary problems if it is short-term—he doesn't carry those on his shoulder. That can lead to letting things build up, which they have. But with God's help, he has faced his weaknesses with courage and walked on.

The scriptures for him are Matthew 5:9 (NASB), Psalm 32:2 (ESV), Jeremiah 17:7 (ESV), Hebrews 6:17–20 (CSB).

> Blessed are the Peacemakers, for they will be called the sons of God.
>
> Blessed is the man against whom the Lord counts no iniquity, and in whose spirit there is no deceit.
>
> Blessed is the man that trusts in the Lord, and whose hope the Lord is.
>
> Because God wanted to show His unchangeable purpose even more clearly to the heirs of the promise, He guaranteed it with an oath, so that through two unchangeable things, in which it is impossible for God to lie, we who have fled for refuge might have strong encouragement to seize the hope set before us. We have this hope as an anchor for our, lives, safe and secure.

Stacy Jean

The language/cultural origin is English.

The inherent meaning is "resurrection" or "one who will be reborn."

The spiritual connotation is "strengthened," which is to make or become stronger and more effective. We most effectively become stronger by facing problems and pressures. To become strong is to achieve control over one's emotions and thoughts and to act bravely and selflessly.

That couldn't fit her more if tried.

I have watched her learn to forgive those who have hurt her. She has also learned to forgive herself by seeing God's heart for her through her failures. She has learned not to absorb the attacks of others and found strength through honesty—as God has said that he desires truth in the inward parts.

That was not an easy lesson to learn. But she has things to teach her children, as she has passionately tried to give them memories and foundations. She knows she will soon have to send them off into a world that is not kind.

The scriptures for her are Psalm 121 (HCSB), Jeremiah 29:11–13 (HCSB).

> Where will my help come from? My help comes from the Lord, the Maker of Heaven and earth. He will not allow your foot to slip; your protector will not slumber. Indeed, the protector of Israel does not slumber or sleep.

The Lord protects you; the Lord is a shelter right by your side. The Lord will protect you from all harm; He will protect your life. The Lord will protect your coming and going both now and forever.

For I known the plans I have for you—this is the Lord's declaration—Plans for your welfare, not for your disaster, to give you a future and a hope.

You will call to me and come and pray to me, and I will listen to you. You will seek me and find me when you search for Me with all your heart. I will be found by you.

Isabel Ruth

The language/cultural origin is Spanish and Hebrew.

The inherent meaning is "consecrated, pledged, or devoted to God," "God is my oath," or "God is abundance."

The spiritual connotation is "discerning spirit"—to be able to see and understand people, things, or situations clearly and intelligently.

From the French, it means "beautiful."

Ruth is a Hebrew name that means a "faithful companion."

She was stunningly beautiful the day she was born with her grandpa Jeff's dark hair. Matthew was in tears that day. Then before we could think, she had a medical issue that put her into the NICU. We were all overwhelmed and stunned with deep concern for our little Izzy! Those days and months were filled with anxiety and with prayers to our loving heavenly Father. There were prognosis given, but God's kindness has overridden the doctor's predictions.

She is the quietest of the girls—a true introvert. I understand and respect who she is. Knowing that underneath that quietness is a girl who thinks deeply and is forming opinions and weighing her steps underneath the surface.

She dances with grace, beauty, and confidence—laying a foundation for the future. She has dreams that are still unformed—hopes for tomorrow. The fog will clear, and she will see clearly.

The scriptures for her are Jeremiah 31:3, 12c, 14b (HCSB), Exodus 15:20–21 (ESV).

> I have loved you with an everlasting love; therefore, I have continued to extend everlasting love

to you—your life will be like a watered garden and my people will be satisfied with my goodness.

Then Miriam the prophetess—took a tambourine in her hand, and all the women followed her with their tambourines and danced. Miriam sang to them: Sing to the Lord, for He is highly exalted; He has thrown the horse and its rider into the sea.

Emerson Jean

The language/culture origin is English.

The inherent meaning is "brave and powerful."

To be brave is to be filled with courage.

To be powerful is to have the ability to control or influence people or things, to have a strong effect.

The nickname *Emmy* means "whole."

The name *Jean* means "God is gracious" and "gifted."

When she was very young, she was quite shy and easily shaken by things. Matthew would play toughen up games and rough her around.

One time, Larry yelled at her because she was on the kitchen table. She made a wide berth around him for quite some time. She later came to love him, after she had toughened up a little.

She is one of the two extrovert grandchildren—Peyton being the other. They have become good friends, and I pray they build a lifelong bond.

She now dances along with her older sister. Sometimes, it is a little harder to be the younger of two sisters—trying to find their own identity.

She is uniquely different and has found herself with grace, beauty, and confidence. We carry the same middle name, which also belongs to her mom and grandmother, Valerie. I always liked being the middle child. I called it being the cream in the middle of an Oreo cookie.

She is a precious young woman.

Scriptures for her are Psalm 20:5 (NIV), 2 Corinthians 2:14 (NASB), 1 John 3:1 (HCSB).

> May we shout for joy over your victory, and lift up our banners in the name of our God.
>
> May the Lord grant all your requests!
>
> But thanks be to God, who always leads us in triumph in Christ, and through us reveals the fragrance of the knowledge of Him in every place. For we are the fragrance of Christ.
>
> Look at how great a love the Father has given to us that we should be called God's children. And we are!

Noah Matthew

The language/cultural origin is Hebrew.

The inherent meaning is "peaceful" and "rest."

The spiritual connotation is "provider of comfort."

Like his father, he arrived unexpectantly—like a gift of love that comes for no apparent reason, as his middle name means, a gift from God. He was an extra blessing and like his father in so many ways. I marvel at this. Children are so often a reflection of us, like a mirror. With Noah, it was a kiss from heaven itself. He is gentle, easygoing, and sensitive to others, as was told earlier of the night that Larry passed away. Instinctively, Noah carefully watched and passed out Kleenex as needed to wipe away tears as they flowed. As I think about this story, I am reminded of a scripture in Revelation 21:4.

It says that God, himself "will wipe away every tear from their eyes." In Noah's heart is a reflection of the heart of God. There is a blessing all around this young man, as he has an ancient ancestor who walked with God.

In Genesis 6:8, the Word of God records that this Noah found grace/favor in the eyes of the Lord. He was a righteous man and was blameless among his contemporaries. He was a man of faith, dependable and unwavering. God could trust him and gave him an assignment. He would build an ark.

Now, lest you dismiss this too quickly, one must keep two things in mind. There was no water around—the ark was built on dry land. The second detail is that building it took 100 years. This was no small or quick task.

God was being patient with sinful man, who at this point in history only did evil—every thought was continually of evil. Then came the miracle of the animals being sent two by two, the flood, and the rainbow. It was the first recorded covenant God made with man. Noah has a rich heritage.

The scripture for him is from the book of Hebrews chapter 8:10–12, 13:20–21 (HCSB).

> But this is the covenant that I will make with the house of Israel after those days, says the Lord: I will put My laws into their minds and write them on their hearts.
>
> I will be their God, and they will be My people, and each person will not teach his fellow citizen, and brother, saying, "Know the Lord," because they will all know Me, from the least to the greatest of them. For I will be merciful to their wrongdoing, and I will never again remember their sins.
>
> Now may the God of peace, who brought up from the dead our Lord Jesus—the great shepherd of the sheep—with the blood of the eternal covenant, equip you with all that is good to do His will, working in us what is pleasing in His sight, through Jesus Christ. Glory belongs to Him forever and ever. Amen.

Mark John

The language/cultural origin is Latin.

The inherent meaning is "martial" or "relating to an army" or "suited for war" or "a warrior."

The spiritual connotation is "strong."

When he was very young, God told me that he would help make our family strong. He has a calling on his life.

The name *John* means "graced by God"—grace and favor are synonymous. God sees him. It also means "strengthened by God." God's strength flows out of our reconciliation with our own weaknesses—something we all must do at some point in our lives.

I actually relate the most with my youngest son. I see him.

When I was a young mother, I learned that the basis of a child's heart was formed in the first few years of their lives, who they really are deep inside—no matter what storms make rock their lives or affect them later. When they become a man—maturity brings changes, but their core still remains deep within. That is why a mother may be separated from them through time or distance, but she still sees their hearts. A mother remembers who they are deep within. She was there.

Mark is a kind and loving and helpful man. He always had an expressed longing for a family and children. He hated being the youngest and watching his siblings get older before him. He was eager to grow up. I was not. He was my baby—and as I so loved my role as a mother. It was very hard to let go. I held on tightly, and I miss those times very much. But loving your children means that you do your job and let them become their own person. Love is not about you; it is about them. They have their own journey through this life, and a mother instinctively knows that.

I have always wanted four children and haven't, for one single moment of time, regretted it, even when I had no idea what I was doing and made countless mistakes.

God never, ever makes mistakes—not with you or your children.

The scriptures for him are Deuteronomy 7:7, 9 (NIV), Deuteronomy 33:27a (ASV), Ephesians 5:1a (NASB).

> The Lord has set His affection on you—know, therefore, that the Lord is a faithful God, keeping His covenant of love to a thousand generations.
>
> The eternal God is your dwelling place, and underneath are the everlasting arms.
>
> Therefore, be imitators of God, as beloved children; and walk in love, just as Christ also loved you and gave Himself up for us.

Jennifer Amy

The language/cultural connotation is Welch and English.

The inherent meaning is "fair one" and "white and smooth" or "white wave."

The spiritual connotation is "trusting."

The inherent meaning of the name *Amy* is "beloved."

From the very beginning of her relationship with Mark, I have been honored to have a young Jewish woman as part of the family. I am intrigued by her heritage and know that God has set his affection on his people. He has set his affection upon her. God blesses those who bless them. It is through this people that God sent a savior to the world to reconcile us and bring peace through his blood for the forgiveness of our sins. It is through them that the wall of hostility between God and man was bridged and we have access to the Father.

She brings a rich heritage to our family. Mark loved her and waited patiently for her during those early years. She has been his heart's desire, and his loyalty is fierce. The deepest longings of her heart are to be loved.

The scriptures for her are Song of Solomon 5:2a, 6–8, 7:10 (ESV), Exodus 33:18a, 19, 34:6–7 (NASB).

> I slept, but my heart was awake. A sound! My beloved is knocking—I opened to my beloved, but my beloved had turned and gone. My soul failed me when he spoke, I sought him, but found him not; I called to him, but he gave no answer.

The watchmen found me as they went about the city; they beat me, they bruised me, They took away my veil. I adjure you, O daughters of Jerusalem, if you find my beloved, that you tell him I am sick with love. I am my beloved's and his desire is for me. I am my beloved's and he is mine.

Moses said, "Please show me Your glory." And He said, "I will make all of my goodness pass before you." The Lord passed before him and proclaimed, "The Lord, the Lord, a God merciful and gracious, slow to anger, and abounding in steadfast love and faithfulness, keeping steadfast love for thousands, forgiving iniquity and transgression and sin."

Alexis Lily

The language/cultural origin is English.

The inherent meaning is "defender" or "helper."

The spiritual connotation is "intercessor" or "one who stands in the gap."

The name *Lily* means "purity" and "shining light."

She was born very early on the day of my mother's last birthday here on earth—May 8, 2014. Alexis remained in the NICU for quite some time, taken great care of and protected with passionate love.

For her tiny size, she caught up quickly—with strength and tenacity. She has acquired this strength from both of her parents. She has a future and a hope, as she grows into the woman she was created to be. Goodness, beauty, and blessing will follow her all the days of her life

The scriptures for her are Psalm 17a, 8 (NASB), Song of Songs 2:2 (NASB), Isaiah 43:1 (ESV).

> Show me the wonders of your great love. Keep me as the apple of your eye; hide me under the shadow of your wings.
>
> Like a lily among the thorns, so is my darling among the young women.
>
> Thus says the Lord he who created you. He who formed you. Fear not, for I have redeemed you; I have called you by your name, you are mine.

WRITINGS FROM VARIOUS TIMES IN MY LIFE

Psalm 23 (KJV):
The Lord is my shepherd—I belong to him.
I shall not want—he takes care of me and provides all that I need.
He maketh me to lie down in green pastures—he gives me rest surrounded by His favor and blessings.
He leadeth me beside still waters—I follow him and have beauty, abundance, and peace.
He restores my soul—he heals me in every place where I have been wounded.
He leadeth me in the paths of righteousness, for his name's sake—he goes before me and shows me the right way to go. I yield to him, and his name is glorified.
Yea, though I walk through the valley of the shadow of death, I will fear no evil, for thou are with me—sometimes, my journey leads me through dark and difficult places, evil whispers to me, but I don't listen because he is holding me with his strong right hand, protecting me, and I know that I am not alone. I am never alone.
Thy rod and thy staff, they comfort me—his promises and presence bring me comfort. They wrap me up close to his heart, and I can hear his heartbeat of love.
Thou preparest a table before me in the presence of my enemies—he prepares a feast, sets a beautiful table, and invites me to dine with him. I enjoy his loving-kindness.
I see him smile at me. He does this with those who are against me, watching—

Thou annointest my head with oil, my cup runneth over—the aroma of his presence floods over my whole being, bringing gladness and healing to every part of my life. This wonder is more than I can contain, and it flows out in abundance.

Surely goodness and mercy shall follow me all the days of my life—the kindness and love of God envelops every moment of my journey here on earth. It is in front of me, behind me—nothing can separate me from it. I trust in him.

And I will dwell in the house of the Lord forever—this life is merely the beginning of all he wants to give me. He has built a home in heaven, and I will live close to him and enjoy his love for all eternity.

Who Are You Following?

Life is designed for us to learn by following our parents. If we, as parents, consider the question or if our parents had, maybe life would have been less of a mystery as we moved into adulthood. Who are you following and why?

Unfortunately, life has a way of keeping us from paying attention to the things that really matter, and many of us have found ourselves on our own with no compass to follow or even understanding that it even matters at all. After all, we are each unique, and there are many paths to follow. They all lead to the same place, don't they? The beauty of life is that we have been given the freedom to make our own choices, as we each have our own unique purposes, which our lives are meant to accomplish. Our lives matter, and it makes all the difference to ourselves and those near us. What we do with our lives has an impact on others, whether we understand that or not. Whether we care to acknowledge it, others are watching and making decisions for their own lives. Someone is following you. Where are you going?

I take my responsibility of parenting quite seriously. Children and grandchildren are a precious treasure of immeasurable value. I could not imagine my life without them, and I am deeply thankful for each and every one of our family. Some of my own intense emotion, concerning my children, has sprung from the struggles I experienced from my own childhood. I had no one to follow or to hold my hand or to tell me my life mattered.

I did not want that for my children or grandchildren. This desire for them to know how loved they are is a passionate, unquenchable flame.

Yet despite my determination, I have had failures that I deeply regret. My hope is that in these issues, I have my children's forgiveness and the recognition by them that they should live their lives differently. I hope they have the wisdom to learn from my mistakes. I do not beat myself up any more about these things, nor do I pretend that they did not happen. The past can never be changed but can be turned around for good if we follow what is right. The error is not in falling down but whether we get up again. It is all about learning. I pray for wisdom and love to fill each of their hearts all the days of their lives. I pray for a determination to learn who to follow and who not to.

I have learned that truth is not truth, just because we want it to be. We do not have the power within our own frail humanity to create truth. Truth will continue to exist without our permission or acknowledgment of such. We have the freedom to believe what we want, but our belief doesn't change what is really true.

Sometimes, we don't like the truth. It can be painful. I am at a point in my life where I will soon be touched by death in some way or another. Death is the last stop in this life and brings us to the end of our freedom to choose. At this moment, I have two aging parents and my aunt and uncle. Death sometimes surprises you. It can come when least expected.

But it will come. Ready or not—I don't like it. It is the last choice—the only one that can never be taken back or undone. Who are you following?

The question is not new, only the understanding that we must answer it. It has always been there in our hearts, yet life has a way of silencing and postponing the response, until we are forced to give an answer. Maybe we fool ourselves into thinking that we don't have to answer, yet the choices we make always reveal what we might not want to admit or face.

If you don't answer with words, your actions always give you away. An extrovert might answer it quickly without considering fully the choice or commitment. Being the introvert that I am, the answer is always slow to come. Yet waiting until I am sixty-one is a rather slow response time, even on my terms. It's important to mean what you say and to say what you mean. That is who I am.

We were very blessed to be able to get away on vacation this last week to a warm place. In February, it is the desire of many who live in Minnesota. I am amazed at the number of people who are able to do this and deeply aware that there are many who cannot. We had a good time, and I am very thankful for the break in the routine of life, for the warm weather and a beautiful place to stay. I am aware that it is a gift. The best gifts are something that you really want but don't expect. To expect something is to think that someone owes you something or that you have somehow earned it. That is not what I am talking about. There is little gratitude in all of that. The best gifts are a surprise. They come with no strings attached. They are things that you will never forget. These are gifts that touch the very core of your being because you know that there is someone who really understands you and loves you. The best gifts teach you to love the giver instead of the gift. They teach you that you are not alone, that you are cherished, and that the deepest longings of your heart are not unimportant. Someone sees you. This time-share is one of those kind of gifts to me. My sister/friend gave it to me.

The biggest surprise of this Florida time is that I came face-to-face with this question. Usually, I would read a book or two, but this time, I just watched movies. There were several good ones, but whether you are reading or watching a movie, you find yourself caught up in the lives of other people—the choices that they made, the life that they had been given. The very best ones are of people who had a purpose and a heart to care for others. It stirs something inside of you. It leaves a question.

Two thousand years ago, Jesus understood that we needed to answer this question. He understood our deepest needs. He gave us a gift. He gave us the answer to the question.

He said, "Come follow me." He didn't ask the question. He just gave the answer.

We all need someone to follow. Without having someone to follow, we would have to figure out all of the answers to life ourselves. Life is too short to make that many mistakes in order to figure out what is really true. I have heard others say, "Truth is whatever you want it to be." Even I know that is foolish. Though I must admit I have been deceived into doing so.

It is not something that you can't recover from, but it can steal years of your life.

So all this is to say, "Who exactly are you following?"

It is a personal question only you can answer. It is a question that an answer must be given—if not now then someday, we all will be required to.

Fear

I have wrestled with fear all of my life, maybe you have too.

There are many issues in life as we journey through—forces that seem too powerful to overcome. Seen or unseen, they are bigger than us.

I could name a few, but it is not necessary, as I know mine, and you know yours.

Looking back on those moments, I realize that it has always been about one thing—learning to trust and be loved by a God I cannot see, learning to not seek rescue, as much as relationship is concerned, not confusing the voices of shame and condemnation that silently shout deep in our souls, with the voice of love that casts out fear, covers our sins, and sympathizes with our weaknesses. In my lifetime, I have probably heard countless teachings about this subject of fear, but I honestly don't remember even one.

What I do remember is what the Holy Spirit has been teaching me. I remember what he has been writing on the tablet of my heart. His words are true. His words are life. His words bring freedom.

I will share a few because I know that he has been teaching you the same.

Isaiah 41:10 reads, "Do not fear, for I am with you; do not anxiously look about you, For I am your God. I will strengthen you, surely, I will help you, Surely I will uphold you with My righteous right hand" (NASB).

Psalm 46:1–2 reads, "God is our refuge and strength, A very present help in trouble. Therefore, we will not fear Though the earth should change and the mountains slip into the heart of the sea" (KJ21).

Psalm 121:2, 5, 7 reads, "My help comes from the Lord. The Lord is thy keeper. The Lord will preserve you from all evil; He will preserve thy soul. The Lord will preserve thy going out and thy coming in from this time forth and even forever more" (KJV).

Do you see it? Do you hear him?

In all these things, he is patiently teaching us not to fear.

But what he is changing *in* us is an unshakable truth.

He is changing us from being fearful to being filled with his strength.

He is placing in our hearts a deep, knowing that he will help us.

There is no trouble or circumstance that is bigger than him.

Today, I am not the same fearful girl that I used to be.

I am not strong because I somehow did something.

I am not strong because I am surrounded by people.

I am strong and fearless because God is for me and with me and in me.

He has been teaching me to believe him when he said, "Do not fear, I am with you, I will strengthen you and I will help you."

The giants that I used to fear are nothing. I don't listen to their whispers anymore.

I have been quieted by his love.

Remember

Deuteronomy 8:2 reads, "You shall remember all the way that the Lord your God has led you" (NASB). It seems to be an issue that I wasn't aware that I had—remembering.

I thought that I did remember, that is. From the time I was very young, there seemed to be a gift of memorizing—words, scriptures, poems, facts, events, whatever—but now, as I look more honestly at this ability to remember, I stand humbled. I have less desire to measure myself with the behavior of others. There is no wisdom in the trap of comparison.

Our only plumb line is Jesus.

But I used to wonder how the children of Israel didn't remember. They seemed to forget so quickly the miraculous deliverance and provision of God—the plagues in Egypt, the pillar of fire, the Red Sea, the wealth and health that they left Egypt with, the manna, the water from the rock, their clothes and shoes not wearing out—like what was wrong with them?

Wouldn't you have loved to have seen those spectacular works of God?

I would! It is easy to judge others, at least I find it easy for me.

Like—really? A golden calf within forty days of Moses being up on the mountain?

And Aaron—he just threw the gold into the fire and out popped a golden idol!

God was not pleased. Didn't they remember?

Why did they forget? I wonder—was it that they didn't understand that God had set his affections on them?

Or did their hearts just still love Egypt?
Did they just want the easy way—without a struggle?
Give me what I want, what I need—life should be easy.
The writer of Hebrews gives us a clue. He said they didn't listen.
They were hardened by sin. We have all been there. I have.

It is human nature to look at what is seen—what we can touch and experience with our senses. Sometimes, we seem to only be concerned about our outward needs. The psalmist tells us that God showed his acts to the children of Israel, but to Moses, he showed his ways.

Moses had a heart to know God.

What is seen is temporal, but what is unseen is eternal.

Understanding God's heart and ways takes looking beyond what is seen. Looking through eyes of faith, believing him, listening with our hearts.

Faith takes remembering—remembering who God is, what he has done, what he has said.

Faith takes earnestly listening—listening and remembering.

Let us be not dull of hearing—we are warned.

Let us take heed and press through with all of our hearts.

I can see clearly, I sin, when I forget. Sin is deceitful like that.

We remember what we want to and truly love.

That is why we need to follow and be like our God and savior. He never forgets—except our sins—if we have accepted his offer of salvation.

God is not like man. God does not forget what we need. God does not forget our afflictions. God does not forget our prayers. God does not forget our tears. God does not forget our good works and love for one another. God does not forget the purposes for which he created us. God does not forget his Word. God does not forget his love for us. God does not forget or change or waiver in his desire for us. God does not forget his children.

Why? The answer is simple. Love does not forget the object of one's affections.

God is love. He loves us—always has, always will.

He remembers all of these because of his great love for us.

"The steadfast love of the Lord never ceases, his mercies never come to an end."

We always remember what we truly love.

Father, change our hearts to love you more than anything else!

Help us love you enough to remember and obey gladly with our hearts.

We are created in your image. We will remember. We will love!

"Bless the Lord, O my soul, and forget not all His benefits."

We will not forget because our eyes are on you, o Lord!

Trust

Joshua 1:5 reads, "I will be with you. I will not leave you or forsake you. Be strong and courageous" (HCSB).

I have to confess that trusting is my greatest weakness. The definition of *trust* is "firm belief in the reliability, truth, ability or strength of someone or something. Confidence, belief, faith, certainty, assurance, conviction, credence, reliance"—that is a mouthful!

I used to trust everyone but learned the hard way—that was not wise. We need to put our trust in something that is trustworthy.

Words mean something. The Word of God is his oath, his promise, his covenant of love. It is the anchor of our souls. Trust in the Lord with all your heart and do not lean on your own understanding. We all know this.

Faith is the substance of things hoped for. Faith takes strength and courage. Faith reveals itself in the actions that we take, in the thoughts that we think, when there is little to hold on to but his promises—not that his promises are little, just unseen, except through the eyes of the Spirit.

We need his help to believe, to see, to adjust our thoughts and actions.

We walk one day at a time, holding on to his hand—really knowing that he is holding on to us.

One scripture that has been written on my heart for many years is from Isaiah 41:9c–14 (ESV):

> I have chosen you and not cast you off; fear not,
> for I am with you; do not be dismayed, for I am

> your God; I will strengthen you, I will help you, I
> will uphold you with My righteous right hand—
> for I the Lord your God, hold your right hand; it
> is I who say to you, "Fear not, I am the one who
> helps you, fear not I am the one who helps you,"
> declares the Lord, your Redeemer.

In a very short space, he says, "Fear not," and "I will help you" three times.

It is like in the New Testament when Jesus repeatedly says, "Verily, verily," or "Truly, truly." He repeats himself because he really wants us to pay attention and believe what he is saying. What he is saying is a sure thing!

Believe me, I need his help! I have learned, after all these years, that I cannot do life without his help. I have tried and failed—miserably!

It is a frightening thing when one has to face that fact—to face one's self. My default is to try and put my trust in someone else—the people around me. It is human nature. Another option is to lie to yourself or drown out the truth by filling your life with noise or addictions or whatever else you choose. They all make the voice inside a little harder to hear. They medicate your soul and make it easier to not deal with and face the truth.

It is easier to hide. Just ask Adam. God was calling, "Where are you? I am here to walk with you. I am here to hold your hand. I am here."

My problem is that I have so easily tried to put my trust in someone else. It shifts the blame off of myself.

If you have had people in your life that have proved faithful, I am very happy for you. I have not. I am quite sure that I am not alone, even though it doesn't feel like it sometimes. I will honestly tell you that I don't like it. I am sure about one thing—it is probably the best thing for me. It forces me to run utterly desperately to God. I do not know if there is anyone who will not leave me. It is all I have ever known (I do not say this out of pity for myself). My hope is in God's mercy toward me.

We were not created to live life alone. It is in our DNA.

I love these words: "*I will be with you.*" I will choose to believe the one who has lovingly never left me, even through the dark and terrifying times of my life.

I look back and see that he not only held my hand but lovingly carried me when I cried and had my hand over my face in the darkness and begged him to take me home.

I have not forgotten those memories. Please don't make me walk through that again! I hear his voice—"*I will be with you. I will not leave you or forsake you.*" My heart desperately clings to these words.

Do not be afraid. Fear is a lie. Love takes it away.

Be strong! Be courageous!

I hear him say, "Be bold! Be confident! I am with you!"

I can choose to remember all those in my life who have left me. It is reality. It happened, and my heart was broken. But through it all, I have learned a critical lesson. He has never abandoned me—never broke his promises. He has always been closer than my breath or heartbeat. He has passionately claimed me as his treasured possession, and no one could ever keep him from breaking his promises to me.

I do not trust in myself. He alone is my strength. And when I wrestle with the issues of this life, he will be for me what I so desperately need. He does not forget us. He has written our names on the palm of his hand. We belong to him—his treasured possession.

Forever loved. Held. Valued. Cherished. Beloved.

The Saints

Psalm 16:3 reads, "As for the saints who dwell in the earth; they are the majestic ones in whom is all my delight" (NASB).

Have you noticed them? I mean, really noticed. I was watching today—faces of beautiful people, majestic people. They are the people who walk in the grace of God. Everywhere I go, I find them. There is this mysterious connection.

The Holy Spirit bears witness. It is the Spirit of Jesus, for his holy presence is living in them and it binds us together. We know them because we know him, and like John the Baptist, who leapt in his mother's womb, the recognition resounds in our hearts. They are the children of God—my brothers and sisters. We have the same heavenly Father. We are family!

I can't help but be amazed at him—my Father, that is! What a good, good Father! We are children born out of love, thought of, and cherished from the beginning of time—planned and wanted.

For many years, I have been overwhelmed by the scripture in Deuteronomy 7 that says he has set his affection upon us. That would be, as the saying goes, "Set in stone"—unchangeable, forever, secure, unmovable!

The word *affection* is beautiful. It carries with it a tenderness, a delight, a deep enjoyment. God doesn't just love us—he likes us! He cherishes us and dances over us with great joy!

This is not a picture of God as the world would define him. If you haven't noticed yet, the world lies. It tells only partial truths, which in essence are lies. Sadly, they just don't know him. I want them to.

Few of the majestic ones would call themselves majestic, but they are different, holy, set apart. When I look at them, I see the reflection of God. I am humbled in their presence and grateful beyond words. I have a family that loves me and a Father that calls me by name. There is a sense of belongingness. We all need that—an identity and connection with the eternal God. We are his! Even though we often forget where we came from.

Most are unaware of the impact that their presence brings. They are off, busy doing the Father's will—each day, taking up the cross, loving, forgetting what lay behind, leaving their labors in the Father's hands to will and to do his good pleasure, and patiently waiting for the seeds to grow, the fruit to ripen, souls to be saved, the kingdom of God to come here on earth as it is in heaven, prayers to see the salvation of our God, the revelation of our Lord Jesus Christ in the lives of a lost and dying world.

But they carry the living God within themselves and the presence of God changes everything. Goodness and mercy chase them down and overtake them. Their cups overflow to all that passes their way. The river of living water floods its banks continually. It changes everything with power, life, and light.

They are blessed in the city, blessed in the country, blessed when they go out and when they come in. They bring light and love and peace to those around them. They carry hope, faith, and love. They are majestic, beautiful, powerful, causing great admiration, respect, dignity, honor, excellence, children of the living God!

The psalmist said that his delight is in them. I can relate. When I look at all of the beauty of creation—the mountains, the oceans, the trees, the meadows and rocks and flowers, the streams, the stars—and think that the very favorite thing God cherished most of all that he has created are people, his children, his beloved, his very own possession—us!

My heart takes great delight in watching, valuing, enjoying, and loving what God loves. His children—they are his!

I Shall Not Be Moved

Psalm 16:8 reads, "I will set the Lord always before me; because He is at my right hand, I shall not be moved" (NASB).

The pronoun *I* is a very personal and singular word. It is not dependent on others, nor is it exerting pressure on others to follow suit.

The word *will* is the mental state by which one deliberately chooses or decides upon a course of action. It is a decision the psalmist made—a declaration of how he would order his life. "I will—"

To *set* is "to put, lay, or stand something in a specific place or position."

It is a bold statement—the determination of where we will choose to give honor and to whom we will give honor to.

The Lord, Jehovah, the master, the one possessing supreme power and authority, the holy one, the Almighty, the Lord of lords, the king of kings. He is the center, the one we choose to place in this position in our lives though our choosing is not the determination of who he is. He is the *Lord*. We are only acknowledging this fact, willingly and humbly submitting to and giving honor to whom it is due. He is the only one, the I AM—savior, redeemer, the prince of peace, wonderful counselor, everlasting Father, everything we ever needed, the one our souls cry out for and will one day bow before.

Always means "always, forever, a holy covenant and commitment." God's covenant is a sure thing—eternal on earth as it is in heaven. He is the security our hearts desperately need and long for. He is not a man that he should ever lie or change.

He is love. He is security. His unchangeable love drives out all fear.

Before me, not after or alongside. He is ahead of us—leading, guiding, protecting. We are following. He is at my right hand. If I see and understand that he is there, my right hand becomes holy because he is holy. The near presence of God changes everything.

He will not let go. Fear is gone. I am not walking alone.

The world—my life becomes different. The touch of the Almighty God, the powerful hand of God, taking my hand and walking through life with me. This bold declaration changes everything. Everything!

I don't know about you, but I like to hold hands with someone I love.

I shall not be move. I am confident. Unafraid. Strong in his care. He is near.

Psalm 23—I just love Psalm 23. Most people do. It could very well be the most-quoted scripture of the Old Testament. Every phrase is packed, full of truth that we desire to embrace and hold dear to our hearts. God's truth is like that. Even when we are far from him, there is something irresistible that draws our hearts to it. There is hope in the words. Our hearts cling to hope—no matter who we are or where we have been. It is in our DNA. In our most dire of circumstances, we grasp on to it. Hope.

Another Psalm says, "Thy word is a lamp unto my feet and a light unto my path" (KJV). We all know that life is a journey. There are many roads or paths for us to choose from.

We have all been given the freedom to choose which path to take. Life has many choices—many decisions we must make. There are decisions we must make, even when we are young or ignorant or feel powerless or totally confused and groping in the darkness. We can even make the decision to do nothing or let someone else decide for us. Our options are many—still, we must make choices. We must choose. There are many of them—choices.

What will I believe? Who will I follow? What will I do for employment? Should I marry and who and when should I marry?

Should I stay married? Should I have children or not? Who will be my friends? Where will I live?

What will I love? Money? Material things? Adventure? Solitude? Beauty? Health? Nature?

Or who will I be? Honest? Kind? Faithful? Trusting? Will I forgive others? Or hold on to anger? Hide behind walls? Self-medicate with addictions of various kinds—food, drugs, alcohol, gambling, sex; the list goes on and on.

Life—our lives are a series of choices that will affect not only the here and now but our end destination. And yes, many of our decisions will be affected by things beyond our control.

Who are our parents and siblings? What is our race or sex or birthplace? Is my family rich, poor, or in the middle? What do we look like? What are our strengths, abilities, talents, or weaknesses? What choices do people around us make that impact our lives? Accidents? Disasters? Difficult situations? Evil? Abuse? Illnesses?

And most important of all—will we choose to believe in God? Does he love me? Is he fair? Can I trust him? Do I believe what he says? Or will we defiantly shake our fists in anger and rebellion against him, either quietly or loudly for all to see?

What will I believe? Who will I believe? Myself? My feelings? Others? Or God?

Where we end up in life will be determined by all of these things—whether we believe it or not. Truth is not what we want to believe is truth. We don't have that power—only God does. But there is good news in all of these things—good news and bad news.

The bad news is that all of us will make wrong choices along our journey of life. Wrong choices that will hurt us and damage our hearts. It is who we are as human beings. Sin is always lurking around us. Whether intentionally or not, we all choose wrong paths at some time. Many of us do it frequently. It will not matter what our motives are—good or evil, the end result will be the same. We find ourselves somewhere we do not want to be, imprisoned by circumstances and our own powerlessness to free ourselves from chains that hold us tightly—chains that hurt us, chains that steal our hope.

Many times, we blame others. Sometimes, we blame ourselves, overcome with shame, guilt, and hatred for ourselves. Sometimes, we give up and think about wanting to end our lives, either actual death or, internally, we let our dreams die. Sometimes, we press on in the darkness, insisting that we have the power and control. But we have forgotten what is really true. Wherever we find ourselves, whatever path we are on is because of a choice or series of choices we have made. It is something that God has given to us—the freedom to choose, freedom to choose life or death.

We all choose death at some point, but the good news is that God will let us choose again. He wants us to choose again. I will say it again—he wants us to choose again.

The good news is that we can turn around and take another path. It is a path that he will make—a path where he will clear away the debris and hopeless wreckage we find ourselves surrounded with. It is a miraculous path that doesn't even exist—until we make a choice to turn our eyes and hearts to the one who created us, who loves us, the one who is the creator of new paths, the one who gave his life so that we could have a path to the one true God. That would be Jesus Christ.

This is really good news—really good news! As I sit here today, as someone who chose many years ago to genuinely surrender my life to God by way of his Son, Jesus Christ, who loved me and died for me, who cleared a path of righteousness that rescued me from certain death. Since that time many years ago, I am well aware that I still have chosen numerous paths along the way and found myself in places that I didn't want to be. Painful places, broken places. And in those places, I found my Father waiting for me to come home back to him. I found him lovingly, patiently leading me in the paths of righteousness for his name sake.

After all, I had become his daughter—and still was his daughter when I made wrong decisions. A loving and just Father does not give up on his children. I learned that through much suffering, through very real circumstances.

When he said, "I will never leave you or forsake you," he didn't lie. Men lie—God doesn't. God never lies. He can't.

My real purpose for writing today is a new awareness of God's relentless determination to lead his children in the path of righteousness, even when they have chosen to take a temporary different path. If he has called you by name and you are his, he will put roadblocks in front of you at every wrong decision you make. He will hedge you in. Don't take my word for it.

You can deceive yourself—but nothing will work or satisfy the longings in your heart. Nothing will hinder him from rescuing you and turning you back home to where you belong. How long it will take you, still, will be your choice.

God never forces anyone to love him. The good news is that from the time you were born, he has been calling your name—whether you have heard it clearly or not or whether you have been covering your ears. In all of life's wreckage, his whisper to your heart continues. When we respond to his voice, repent of our decisions to do things our own way, God himself will call things into being that do not presently exist. He will create, out of nothing, paths of righteousness for his name's sake—green pastures and still waters, paths that restore our souls. This is good news! This is a foundation for hope.

It is a path worth choosing—

Waterfalls

Psalm 42 reads, "Deep calls to deep at the roar of your waterfalls; all of Your breakers and your waves have gone over me" (ESV).

I read a book several years ago called, *the Sacred Romance* by John Eldridge. It resounded in my soul. I clearly saw how the living God had set romance in my heart from the beginning. Like a picture on a movie screen, I could not turn away from the one who would so relentlessly pursue me with so great a love.

We were created for beauty, adventure, and romance. My heart knew that very well from a young child.

I found myself on the island of Maui. It was a gift from a friend—a place to stay, to rest, to be free for a moment from things to come. My heart danced with excitement and eager anticipation. Before me was beauty, adventure, and romance with the lover of my soul. It was the true me that few have seen or known.

I smile at the thought of it. The memory still plays with great joy in my heart—even now! I could have been in heaven. It was a momentary glimpse. Like a child, I played for three weeks.

I was lured by my heart off the beaten path. The mountain river was running low, and I found myself being drawn to the singing—the earth, the water, the rocks all chorused praise, joy, and inexpressible laughter. And me—just me and God. Oh, let me stay and just be! Just a little while longer! Yes! Yes! My heart sang—

I got into the water and began to climb over the rocks, following the river, up the mountain. The rocks were of all sizes. Some slippery with moss and algae but welcoming and inviting me to stay and listen—listen and learn. I heard a song. My heart knew the melody.

Worship—the worship of the king of kings. All of creation knows it. That day, the sound of his voice was all I heard. Sweetly deafening. Roaring.

Somehow, it is in our nature to try to escape and resist hardships. Our hearts cry out, "Teach us your ways, O Lord. help us to know you. Make us like you. Give us love and patience."

He hears our prayers and sends us lessons we need to learn.

Lord, may we see that it is in the placing of the rocks in our lives that the river sings. Without the rocks, the water wouldn't sing and dance. You have seen the quiet river. He leads us beside still waters. We need that too, as his love quiets our soul.

But we need the joy-filled dancing waters that rejoice and sing as our God brings us through deep waters. We find that he never lets the waters flood over our heads. He brings us through and carries us through the deepest waters.

We can never learn that he is our savior unless we are deeply aware that we need to be saved. The deep waters do that.

That day was not enough for my heart. I needed more. The mountains have always called my name. The call is deep and clear and unmistakable—that of Mount Zion, the mountain of the Lord, the city of the great king. Her highway runs through my heart—always has, always will. I just had to sleep up in the mountain by the waterfall I had found.

It rained the next day. The river was raging well over the banks from the day before. They say that IAO has as much rain as 300 inches every year. The river floods as the water comes rushing down its steep slopes—wild, exciting, dangerous!

I couldn't climb the way I had the day before—through the mountain forest I went, forging on, drawn by love, beauty, adventure, romance.

I climbed until I found my waterfall! The rocks were well under water. It was the mighty sound of the power of sheer water that gave praise to the Lord that summer night. All of his creation sings his name—even when no one hears.

But I heard that night, and the sound was deep calling to deep. My heart knows the song well. In the midst of danger, there is safety.

He watches—smiling, protecting, holding me, singing his song of love over me. The stars twinkled and winked that night. We had a secret. God speaks our love language. He wrote it on our hearts.

All your breakers and your waves have gone over me, o Lord!

The Mountains

Psalm 48:1 reads, "His holy mountain, beautiful in elevation, is the joy of the whole earth, Mount Zion...within her citadels God has made Himself known as a fortress" (ESV).

These words stir my heart deeply—holy mountain, beautiful, joy of the whole earth.

To those who dwell within her citadels, he is a fortress! He is our fortress!

Mount Zion is the place of holiness, beauty, joy, strength, and safety! It is the dwelling place of God!

The definition of *citadel* is "the smaller part of the city that is the strongest part of the defense system, the defensive core, the fortified center." A *fortress* is "a military stronghold—heavily protected, impenetrable, or a person or thing not susceptible to outside influence or disturbance."

Do you see what God is saying? He has made himself known. He has revealed himself as our fortress. Nothing can penetrate his protection that we are surrounded by. In his presence, we are safe. There is complete and utter safety within his citadels.

Father, open our eyes and our hearts to know in the depths of our beings that we are safe—forever! You are our fierce protector! An impenetrable shield and defender.

I have believed the lies of the enemy. I have been deceived. I have said in my heart, "I am not safe. There is no one to protect me." I have looked to man as a hero, and there was no one—none—to stand as a warrior, none who understood.

Oh, the foolishness of it all! The futility of being rescued by a stone idol. The incredible foolishness. An idol has no power for even a moment. I repent.

How could I ever put my trust in those who cannot save themselves, no less me? You shall know the truth, and the truth shall set you free. Freedom brings *joy*!

Freedom breaks the chains, opens prison doors, releases captives from bondage and slavery, heals broken hearts, and brings hope, light, and life. Freedom sets your feet to dancing. It was fulfilled as Jesus stood in the temple and read out of the book of Isaiah that Sabbath day.

My heart always longed for a safe place, a shelter from the enemy. It has been a deep need—one that I cannot shake. Zechariah prophesied "that we would be saved from our enemies and from the hand of all who hate us, and that we being delivered from the hand of our enemies might serve him without fear in holiness and righteousness all the days" (ESV). Our safety is not just for our eternal homes one day—it is for now. As the mountains are round about Jerusalem, so the Lord is round about his people forever!

Mount Zion is a place of beauty. It is a place of great joy and utter safety—for he is there!

Angels

Psalm 91:11 reads, "For he will command His angels concerning you to guard you in all your ways" (ESV). There was an angel around me last night. I didn't see it with my eyes, but in my spirit, I did. It was large, and the feathers on his wings were spread out like a comforting shield, encircling my car. I could feel his presence. I wasn't in danger from harm—I was safe.

He was a reminder that I was not alone. We are never alone. The Holy Spirit dwells within us, and Jesus has promised that he would never leave us or forsake us, but sometimes, our eyes are open to see or know with a little extra awareness. We are not alone. The writer of Hebrews tells us that angels "are ministering spirits sent out to serve for the sake of those who are to inherit salvation." They are there.

As I have said, I was not in danger that I was aware of. I am (was) traveling by myself on a road trip to Colorado—my first trip since my husband went home to be with the Lord. It was my first driving trip—alone. There is no issue or fear of being the sole driver, no fear or concern that all will go well. I am well provided for—just one night in a parking lot, sleeping in the back of my car. I could have gotten a motel room—I didn't.

I do not have many experiences or awareness of the presence of angels in my life, though there is no doubt they are always near. My sister had a powerful experience one time while driving from Minnesota to Illinois in the winter one year. She was on 94, traveling south on the divided highway. When she looked up and saw the traffic traveling north, suddenly, an accident occurred. The car hit and began to flip over and over in the air, moving in the direction of the lanes she was in. It was coming straight toward her. It stopped within feet from her car. She knew clearly that an angel had stood between the car and her. I have had no miraculous experience such as this. My stories are few—two more to be exact.

It was in 1976, and I had just recently given birth to Matthew David. The name *Matthew* means "gift from God," and *David* means "beloved." After Matthew was born, I found that the name also means "recompense"—to pay back for damage done or hurt received. He was a timely gift to me. It was a fearful time in my young life. During the pregnancy, I found that my marriage was in serious trouble. I only really realized this after Matthew had been born.

I had three young children—no way of taking care of them by myself. It left me heartbroken, rejected, fearful. You get the picture. I cried and cried after he left that night, which was a normal occurrence. As I was alone in the dark, I became acutely aware that I was not alone.

There were two angels standing at the foot of the bed, one in each corner, like sentinels standing guard—not protecting me, just watching over me, reminding me that there is more than what we see with our eyes. That was forty-one years ago. Their presence was so real that it is as though it happened yesterday. Time with God is a funny thing. There is no forgetting when God does something, says something, opens your eyes to the truth. It is very personal and becomes stamped into the very core of your being.

My second experience with angels happened when the home I lived in, in Minnetrista flooded our walkout basement. I worked for hours, carrying out gallons and gallons of water that day. I was exhausted. After several hours, it was getting dark, and I tried to carry the water far enough away from the house that it wouldn't add to what was saturating the floor. As I took another bucket of water out and turned around, I tripped on the step. I should have fallen and would have hurt myself badly but something caught me and held me upright. I knew instantly that an angel had kept me from falling.

The scripture from Psalm 91 (KJV) filled my heart: "They shall bear you up in their hands, lest you dash your foot upon a stone."

I don't know why we trip and fall sometimes, but that night, I was caught and held. I remember being held.

I remember my first little stepdaughter, Alyssa. She was precious beyond words to me. Her mom let me have her every weekend for many months. There was a deep bond between us. I would walk in the door, and her eyes would light up. She would lift her arms to me, and I could have never ever refused to lift her up into my arms. One day, the Lord used that as an illustration to my heart. He said, "If you raise your arms to me, I will always pick you up and hold you close to my heart."

Always. Always be held. I raise my arms, my heart to you!

Deuteronomy 33:27 says, "The eternal God is your dwelling place, and underneath are the everlasting arms" (ASV).

Psalm 91: 4 says, "He will cover you with His feathers, and under His wings you will find refuge; His faithfulness is a shield and rampart" (NIV).

Fix Our Eyes

Psalm 123:1–2c reads, "To you I lift up my eyes, O You who are enthroned in the Heavens!

Our eyes look to the Lord our God, until He has mercy upon us" (ESV).

The Bible instructs us to fix our eyes on Jesus.

I am sure that you have noticed that wherever you go, you travel in the direction that your eyes have focused on. It will be as sure as the gravity that pulls you to the earth. Where you choose to turn your eyes, look at, gaze upon will be the direction that your feet will travel in life. Now I am not talking about a glance—we all see things we would rather not follow, as we do live in this world, but where we fix our eyes determines where our hearts will go.

As I reflect on my life, I know it has happened every time in my life. Though we may or may not believe this truth, I have found that. If I am honest with myself, there have been times that I have turned my eyes away and ignored this. I have become a forgetful hearer and not a doer. I have looked in the mirror and then gone on my way, forgetting because that was what my heart wanted. Our eyes are directed by the desire of the heart.

Jesus tells us much about our eyes in the sermon on the mount. In chapter 5, he tells us that if our eye causes us to sin by looking at things that lead us to sin, we would be better off without it than to let it lead you to hell.

Again in verse 22, Jesus declares, "The eye is the lamp of the body."

If our eye is good—in the Greek, it means "unwilling to do harm, without guile, sincere, genuine, pure, benevolent, kindly." The results in our whole body, being full of light. If our eye is bad—in the Greek, it means "absence of light, spoken of persons in moral darkness." If this is our state, Jesus declares, "How great is the darkness!"

Our eyes reveal our hearts—which leads to life or death. What you choose to look at with your eyes will produce fruit—good or bad. What you watch, what you read, what you envy will produce lightness or darkness, life or death. Do not be deceived—choose light and flee darkness.

Seek him. Turn your eyes upon Jesus! As the song says, "Look full in His wonderful face. And the things of earth will grow strangely dim, in the light of His glory and grace." The most important eyes are the eyes of the Lord! He sees it all—everything!

Proverbs 15:3 says, "The eyes of the Lord are in every place" (KJV).

Second Chronicles 16:9 says, "The eyes of the Lord move to and fro throughout the Earth that He may strongly support those whose heart is completely His" (NASB).

Psalm 33:18 says, "Behold the eye of the Lord; on those who hope for His lovingkindness" (NASB).

Psalm 34 says, "The eyes of the Lord are toward the righteous and His ears are open to their cry" (NASB).

God is looking with his eyes for those who are looking for him. Strong support hope, powerful, earth-shattering when our eyes meet his eye to eye in agreement and faith.

Psalm 17:8 says, "Keep me as the apple of Your eye; hide me in the shadow of Your wings" (NASB).

More Than the Sand

Psalm 139:17–18 reads, "How precious to me are your thoughts, O God! How vast is the sum of them—they are more than the sand" (NASB).

I have to admit that the first time I heard God speak to me, I fell in love. It wouldn't have mattered what he said to me. I was desperately needing what he had to give me.

We love him because he first loved us. His love is always first. Love begins with him.

He loved me long before I knew it actually, from the foundations of the world. He loved me and was watching over me when I was a very young girl. I wandered through the fields, climbing up trees in search of bird nests, picking wildflowers, dancing in the tall grass, and just loving life. At that point, there was little fear.

I didn't know him, but he knew me. He had called me by my name and had written a book about all my days here on earth. He saw me. In a world full of people that he loved, I was not too small for him to notice. Nothing will ever surprise him, but I didn't know this. There is too much we don't know. There is so much he wants us to know and so much he wants to give to us.

But again, I didn't know—I was just a little girl. He knew that too.

The foundation was laid, and the wonder of life was planted—then came the fire and the fear, and my little girl's life was shaken. Our home burned to the ground when I was six. We moved into the big city. Almost all I had was gone—just like that.

I didn't know that the father I adored didn't love my mother or me. I only saw small signs that he wouldn't keep his promises. It is good to not know some things when you are little—that was sixty years ago, and some days, I still feel small.

But God knows all things, and my life's journey would be with him. He has told me that my name is written on the palm of his hand—his righteous right hand.

I am safe, but I don't always feel that way. He says that love casts out all fear. I do not say I have arrived. I choose day by day. Some days, I forget and I need a reminder. I panic and let fear creep in—his word brings peace when I believe it. I am comforted that the truth of who he is doesn't change with my ability to believe. My Father doesn't change or waver because of my weaknesses. In him, I am strong. In him, I have safety. In him, I can rest. I am in him, and he is with me—such a mystery!

Jeremiah 31:2b (KJV) reads, "I have loved you with an everlasting love, with lovingkindness I have drawn you." Kindness draws me like a magnet—just let me sit with you awhile. Love—how do I understand such tangible things? God loves the whole world.

I get lost in a crowd. Do you see me? I remember Elizabeth Barrett Browning's poem from the eighteenth century:

> How do I love thee? Let me count the ways. I love thee to the depth and breath and height my soul can reach, when feeling out of sight for the ends of being and ideal grace. I love thee to the level of every day's most quiet need, by sun and candle light.
>
> I love thee freely, as men strive for right. I love thee purely as they turn from praise.
>
> I love thee with passion put to use in my old griefs, and with a love I seem to lose with my lost saints. I love thee with the breath, smiles, tears of all my life; and if God choose I shall love thee better after death.

Human love is fragile. I dare not put my trust in it. The psalmist said, "Your thoughts of love for me are more than the sands of the sea." If I should count them, would that help me understand? So I did count some, that is. He knew that I needed to count. That is just who I am—counting, counting. I found that there are more than fifty thousand grains of sand per tablespoon. God's thoughts of love for us are more than all the sands of the sea! My brain cannot comprehend such wonder! Can it be true!

I think that my heart has been measuring love from the wrong source.

God's love is unseen, except through faith—or is it everywhere I look? It surrounds me in all of nature and all of the goodness he has so kindly blessed me with. His presence and love flood my very being. My heart knows it well—like a lover, I am satisfied yet ever hungry for more.

The Path of the Righteous

Proverbs 4:18 reads, "The path of the righteous is like the light of dawn, which shines brighter and brighter until full day" (NASB).

Before I share what is on my heart, I find myself needing to preface this with the statement: I have had trouble viewing myself as righteous. I sometimes cringe when I read, in the psalms, David declaring, "The Lord rewarded me according to my righteousness" (NASB). I have, most of the time, tried to be good—but righteous? I have failed miserably in my own flesh. I am learning not to look at myself through my own eyes but, rather, through my Father's eyes. He sees something entirely different. He calls me righteous in Jesus—holy, chosen, beloved.

The path of the righteous—

I am hiking in the mountains today. Alone yet not even remotely alone. My Father is with me. I am being very still. He has much to say and show me.

I am listening, not to the trees and wind—they are loud high in the mountains—but to his quiet voice deep within my spirit. My feet are moving, but my heart is listening intently.

We have all said it—life is a journey, a path. The destination is of utmost importance; after all, eternity is forever, and our days here are but a breath. How we travel will make all the difference.

As for me, my life is like hiking in the mountains. If you have never been there, I encourage you to go. If your life, like mine, is a path through the mountains, you must stay alert—there are many devices of the evil one lying in wait to trip you up. I speak from experience. But the ways of God are illustrated everywhere. And I wouldn't trade my journey through the mountains for any other way.

God's ways and plans for us are perfect! In the mountains, the path is often steep. The air is thinner, and as you ascend, your heart beats faster. You must look ahead but also at your feet. The path twists and turns constantly. The view is limited to short distances. On the ground, boulders, rocks, and roots are everywhere. Some are firmly planted; others shift and move under your feet. One needs to pay attention—there is danger of tripping. I notice that many use walking sticks to steady their steps.

Most people do not travel alone, but some do. They respond with a smile, a greeting, some even with a conversation but then go on their way. Besides the rocks and roots, some areas are shaded with trees. They are ever reaching for the light, but under their cover is shade. It is cooler there, and in the dappled shade, small flowers grow.

There are also remains of the past—old dead logs strewn and rotting from a time long gone. One wonders of the days of their glory. They, too, reached for the heavens and declared the glory of God. Their voice is silent now, but new growth bursts forth—always. Nature will always reach for him, and men will always search.

The voice of God is always calling. The path of the righteous is ordered by the Lord. He leads us in the path of righteousness for his name's sake. As for me, I would have chosen a smooth, flat path—the easy way—but my heart has always heard the call of the mountains, brighter and brighter. It echoes in my being. "Come higher my daughter, let your feet be like hind's feet. Do not let the twists and turns delay your climb. Do not let the steepness frighten or hinder your steps. Do not stop your feet from moving ever upward. Do not stand still—keep moving. My voice will get clearer and clearer. You are not alone. I am watching, smiling, waiting."

One can get lost in the mountains. I did today, briefly. I took a wrong turn. There was a *Y* in the path and a large group of people deciding which way to go. I decided to avoid them. My decision to look at them turned me onto the path that was not leading me where I was headed. Fear of man can lead you astray. I traveled a long way.

My heart told me I should head down, and the path was strangely quiet with no other travelers. I prayed.

I knew God was near, but it was getting late, and I was tired after walking twelve miles that day. For only a moment, I was afraid, but wisdom whispered to me, "Travel back—retrace your steps. You are not alone."

He is ever with me, and those who love me are praying.

No fear. He has ordered our steps, and though sometimes we lose our way and grow weary, he is holding our hand. He has a righteous right hand, and his loving-kindness will never let us travel the wrong way for long.

The path of the righteous is like the light of dawn, which shines brighter and brighter until the full day. As we get closer and closer to the end of our journey, hear his voice is clearer, sweeter, ever protecting, lovingly guiding, ever calling us upward. Bright and clear is his voice that beckons us to keep on the path that draws us ever homeward. Someday, that is where I will be—home.

Yet I know that I still have some distance to travel. I will enjoy my hike up the mountain of the Lord. He has much yet to show me and whisper in my ear.

Daddy, I am eagerly listening.

A Watered Garden

Jeremiah 31:12c, 14b reads, "Their life shall be like a watered garden, and My people shall be satisfied with My goodness, declares the lord" (NASB).

I love gardens! I love plants and flowers and trees! I am not alone—God does too!

It is good to love what God loves. Can you imagine? Genesis 2 tells us, "And the Lord God planted a garden. The Lord God made to spring up every tree that is pleasant to the sight and good for food. A river flowed out of Eden to water it" (ESV).

I want to see the Garden of Eden! I really do! Pleasing to the sight, beauty beyond words, uniquely different shapes and sizes, colors vibrant like rainbows that you could touch and smell and gather in bouquets, springs flowing, water dancing, birds singing, leaves rustling in the breeze.

Oh, let me sit in the middle of his garden! Let me breathe in deeply with unimaginable pleasures, flooding all of my senses. Like I said, my heart longs to earnestly see and be in the garden that God created.

My heart yearns for one other experience. The scriptures tell us that the Lord God walked in the garden in the cool of the day. Something so wondrous needs to be shared with those you love.

The gift of sharing cannot be underestimated. Together—not alone—my heart yearns to walk with him, the master gardener, the creator of all that is beautiful, good, and pleasant. Teach me, Lord. Hold my hand and let me be in your presence. Let me hear your voice and speak to me. Isn't that why I was created—to know you, to walk with you?

The chief end of man is to glorify God and enjoy him forever! It is also what eternal life is all about. Jesus said in John 17, "And this is eternal life, that they know You the only true God, and Jesus Christ whom You have sent" (ESV).

Eternal life is knowing the true God, who made the heavens and the earth and the first garden.

But I have somehow found myself alone at times. I do not like this. I resist it and find myself pushing against the circumstances of life. There are days that I am not satisfied and I struggle—I wrestle with myself and God. I don't mean to be this way, and I am sorry. Be thankful. Trust God. Live loved. I try to be good, but sometimes, I am just lonely. I can't let others know this. It is not good for man to be alone. I have a hard time accepting this. The pressure presses in on my soul.

My heart cries out. I turn my face with tears to him. The tears run down—stream down. Will they ever stop? Do you see? Will you please just hold me? Daddy—

Then he whispers again to me—the voice I so desperately wait for. His footsteps—I hear him. I do not want to hide. I wipe my tears away, but he knows they were there. There is nothing he hasn't seen or known. There is no hiding. His arms are around me and bring comfort, safety, and hope. I nestle in deeply, knowing that, in all of my weaknesses, I am loved.

I really never was all alone. He whispers, "You are my garden. Beautiful, fragrant, uniquely created by my hand to bring forth my glory. You are my fragrance, my color, my hand, my love. No one else could be or do what I fashioned you for. No one else could sing your song or tell your story."

I hear the music—the notes play quietly upon my soul the old hymn written by Charles Austin Miles in 1912. The story is told that he had a vision in which he saw Mary, weeping in the garden—the tomb was empty, her heart was broken, then Jesus spoke her name: "Mary."

I wait to hear you call my name. I know that you know it. Your eyes are upon me. Your ears are listening. I turn my head toward you. Let me hear and listen gain.

> I come to the garden alone, while the dew is still on the roses and the voice I hear, falling on my ear, the Son of God discloses.
>
> And He walks with me and He talks with me and He tells me I am His own; and the joy we share, as he tarries there, none other has ever known.
>
> He speaks and the sound of His voice, so sweet that the birds hush their singing and the melody that He gave to me, within my heart is ringing.
>
> And he walks with me and He talks with me and he tells me I am His own; and the joy we share as he tarries there, none other has ever known.
>
> I'd stay in the garden with Him, though the night around us is falling, but He bids me go, through the voice of woe, His voice to me is calling.
>
> And he walks with me and He talks with me and he tells me I am His own; And the joy we share as he tarries there, none other has ever known.
>
> Come away my Beloved. Let us sing and dance—together.
>
> In my garden of love, I am satisfied with your goodness.

Wait for Him

Lamentations 3:25 reads, "The Lord is good to those who wait for Him; to the soul who seeks Him" (NASB).

We've all said it. "God is good—all the time! All the time—God is good!" I know it to be true, but sometimes, it is hard to believe.

Unless one is born again, Jesus said, "You cannot see the kingdom of God." It can be hard to believe if one cannot see. It can be hard to see if one is blind. That is why the world attributes and blames God for all the evil that happens.

How could God let this happen? We have all thought it.

We have all experienced Martha and Mary's hearts. "If only you had been there, Lord. Lazarus wouldn't have had to die! You could have stopped this from happening!" We have all pointed the finger at God.

These are all actually lies and tricks the devils use to keep you from running to God. The truth is that Lazarus did die—but he lived. There was a resurrection! Jesus used his death to illustrate truth. He does that in all of our lives, too.

As his daughter, I know it to be true. God is good—always! Yet at times, I have not always felt so good. I have found that my feelings are not a reliable source of truth, nor do they always see and reflect his goodness. I don't want that to be my reality.

As I look and meditate on this scripture, I see something new. Here it is—God has extra goodness for those who wait for him. There is something worth waiting for; there is something worth seeking. There is something worth hoping for! God takes great delight in those who turn their hearts to him, those who search for him and patiently wait, knowing that there is good coming. God is saying, "Wait for it! Put your hope in me. You will not be disappointed!"

I don't know about you, but that makes me excited! Maybe I am easily excitable! Truth about my Father is exciting! Yet waiting can be very hard—very hard! During the waiting time, it is so easy to forget, and the enemy of our souls keeps whispering, "Did God really say that? Maybe he changed his mind? Maybe he is sleeping or forgot you or has more important things to do or people to keep him busy? Maybe he lied."

Whatever the lie that creeps in may be, it is easy to doubt. Yet the waiting time is a testing time. It is good for us. It is good for us to wait. There, I said it! *Good for us to wait!*

I don't know what crowd you hang out with, but I have heard much talk about patience. Don't pray for patience, they say! God will answer and give you all kinds of things to be patient about. We want patience yet run from the process of forming it in our hearts. We are impatient about learning patience—how funny are we?

What we need is to learn God's ways. If you haven't noticed, he is not in a hurry. God is patient with us, and that is a very good thing. We are slow learners. Love is patient and kind. That is what God is and what he illustrates.

And so, we wait—not with hopelessness or frustration or doing nothing, waiting for time to pass. But with eager expectation, we search the horizon like a bride waiting for her groom. We wait and rest, knowing he will come.

We look. We long. We dream! Our hearts cry, "Come soon, Lord!"

I know now that it is good for me to wait for God. It is good to seek him. This makes him smile.

Jeremiah prophesied that God's people would "come and sing aloud on the heights of Zion, and they would be radiant over the goodness of the Lord—that we would be satisfied with his goodness!"

I don't know about you, but to shine with the goodness of the Lord is worth waiting for!

The Wilderness

Hosea 2:14–15a reads, "Therefore, behold, I will allure her and bring her into the wilderness, and speak kindly to her. And there I will give her her vineyards and make the Valley of Achor a door of hope" (NASB).

One must carefully look at the meanings of these words to even remotely begin to understand the unspeakable heart of God. As I ponder the overwhelming impact of what God has declared over us, the tears roll down my face with deep gratitude and humility. I never dreamed of the possibility or of the depth of such love.

The word *behold*, at first glance, appears to be insignificant. Yet as the meaning behind it becomes apparent, my heart stops when I hear the Holy Spirit whisper, "Observe with care! Gaze upon what I am going to show you! Look! This is remarkable! Impressive! More wonderful than you ever dreamed or imagined! Remarkable, impressive, beyond wonder!" The tears flow down—

The word *allure* is the quality of being powerfully and mysteriously attractive. That is what God is! I attest to the power of the unspeakable love of God! He is like a magnet my heart is drawn and pulled to. I cannot escape this heart I am tethered to. I do not want to, nor can I. I do not want to run from the very one who truly loves me. My heart follows him into the wilderness, like one who has blinders on, eyes fixed straight ahead.

The wilderness is not a place that allures us. It is an uninhabitable and inhospitable environment. It is not a place that we would choose to go to, but it is a place that I have found myself—a necessary place. I am easily distracted, so to get my attention, I am drawn away, allured by the love of God.

The wilderness is a lonely place—ugly, barren, a place where I must face myself with all of my weaknesses, all of my sin, and my inability to break its power over me (everything that I don't want to be).

God has turned the Valley of Achor into a door of hope, not in me but the one who loves me. To comprehend the implications of such a miraculous thing is to know that the Valley of Achor is a place of trouble, a place of death, a sentence of death because of sin. The wages of sin is always death—a place of deserved judgment, a stoning. Achan and his family were stoned to death for hidden sins. Nothing is hidden from God. Before we can ever embrace the power of mercy, we must face judgment.

Facing judgment reveals and unlocks the beauty of mercy. When I have forgotten and I have turned to other idols, remind me. Remind me once again who I am to you, oh lover of my soul! Nothing else could ever satisfy. I need your forgiveness!

Take me away with you. In your presence, the wilderness becomes beautiful! Allure me. Bring me. Speak kindly to me! Speak gently! In the wilderness, I listen better. Your voice is clearer.

Tell me that you have betrothed me to you forever! Speak to me in words that I understand. Show me your love. You speak my love language. You gave it to me.

Tell me that I am betrothed to you in righteousness, in justice, in loving-kindness and compassion, in faithfulness! Let me know you. Let me see you, you who my soul loves! Do not hide yourself from me!

Remember that it was in the wilderness that God brought forth water from a rock—streams in the desert! It is in the wilderness that his branches will spread and his splendor will be like an olive tree, his fragrance like the forests of Lebanon. It is his fragrance that we follow into the wilderness and find that he has made an eternal covenant through the blood of Jesus—to betroth us to himself!

How can we resist such love as this!

You Love Him

First Peter 1:8 reads, "Jesus Christ, though you have not seen Him, you love him" (NASB).

I asked someone lately what God did to turn his heart to love him. I didn't just mean believe in him—I meant *love* him. It was a fair question, just not one that can be answered quickly. I couldn't even answer that question, right then, myself. I would need time to wrestle with it and search my heart. To look at the fierce, vast love of God for us—so immense that we would love, more than anything, someone we cannot even see. Peter testifies. "Though you do not see Him, you love Him." It is true, but how did this happen? The simple answer could be because he first loved me, or maybe because he died for my sins, or he forgave me. In honesty, I was glad that he didn't try to answer my question at that moment.

There is a song out recently that says, "I know you are able, and I know you can save through the fire with your mighty hand, but even if you don't—my hope is you alone." How does one get to the place that you love someone that much? That you would place all of your hope in him, even in the fire?

That word *fire* makes us all uncomfortable. I have been reading in Job this week. It begs the question, Do we love God for *what* he has done *for* us or is doing for us? or because of *who* he is? It is a divided question—a hard question. Job answered too quickly and had to repent.

Don't answer too quickly. How do we know and love him without using the circumstances of our lives as a measuring stick of his love for us? How do we go from broken, fearful creatures to children who have no fear, trusting confidently, loving him, steadfast, even in the fire? There is no simple answer—

We all love the stories of the end blessings of Job, of David and Goliath, of Daniel in the lion's den, and of Shadrach, Meshach, Abednego, and the fiery furnace. They are pictures of God's magnificent and powerful deliverance of those who believed in him during the fire.

But what of the prophets, who longed to see the salvation of the Lord? They lived all of their lives seeing God's promises from afar.

God's love leaves us footprints in his Word, examples of those who, through faith and patience, received his promises and of those who only saw through the eyes of faith. They saw what cannot be seen with the human eye. They believed.

That seems to be the word I am searching for. They saw something. They saw God. But how do we see something that our natural eyes can't see?

As I was hiking around a lake this morning, the answer came. There is a deep sense of longing for God in my heart up in the mountains. It is in the beauty, his splendor, his power. They are an illustrative masterpiece that he has signed. The mountains are a place where the noise of this world cannot drown out the song of his love so easily. His voice speaks clearly when one is alone and listening. The world is so noisy. Sometimes, it is hard to think or hear. I heard him this morning. He answered my question. We see him because he reveals himself to us. The secrets of the kingdom of God are given to us. Christ is in us, and we are in him—a mystery, a miracle!

The Holy Spirit is our teacher, the revealer of God. Jesus spoke in parables and stories because, in seeing, the people did not see and, in hearing, the people didn't hear, nor did they understand. But to those who receive him, he is the power of God. The king of kings, the only true God dwells within us! The Holy Spirit illustrates truth and teaches us. He writes truth in our hearts. Just as God knows our different love languages, he also knows our different ways of learning. He speaks in words, actions, pictures, illustrations, circumstances of our lives—our part is to hear, believe, receive because there will always be a test.

The Word of God is tested and proven. Peter tells us in that same passage:

> Though now for a little while, if necessary, you have been grieved by various trials, so that the genuineness of your faith, which is more precious than gold that perishes though it be tested by fire, may be found to result in praise and glory and honor at the revelation of Jesus Christ.

A fire is never fun—never ever. It burns up and wipes away everything that is perishable. Fire proves the heart, our faith—it purifies us. Cleanses. I have loved the blessings of God in my life. There have been plenty, and he is good. But love is not measured in blessings but by faith in him and who he is, not what he does.

My answer to the question is he was there in and after the fire. I saw him, his heart, his love. It was then that I loved him.

At what place and time did you did you fall in love with Jesus?

Even Jesus asked Peter, "Do you love me?" Jesus asked Peter three times.

He is asking you and me—

Father, I confess that I have loved many other things in my life, but none of them compare to your great loving-kindness. I see you, and now, I love you—your daughter.

My Retirement

Time is an amazing but mysterious gift we all possess. Amazing, as it equalizes all of us, whether young or old, rich or poor, educated or not—with twenty-four hours each day to choose how we will experience life. Time is mysterious because, at one moment, we are holding a crying infant and time feels like minutes are hours without end, then we turn around and are celebrating their graduation or marriage. How do these things happen? Amazing—mysterious!

I feel that way about my job at the post office in Maple Plain. These thirty years have been rich in experience, friendship, and enjoyment, but how have they slipped by so quickly? Am I really this old—really?

As many of you know, after delivering mail out of Maple Plain since 1984, I will be retiring on December 26. With me will go many, many memories and much history that will no longer be held dear, except in my heart. Nostalgic as I am, I cannot leave without making an effort to share them with anyone who will listen. I cannot walk away silently, as if none of it mattered. It does. Our lives all matter. Someone else will do the job, and it will become their life, but that does not erase or replace what has been done or who we are. The old does not become obsolete, rather a precious foundation upon which our lives have been built.

I would like to first pay tribute to the three men who delivered mail at the time I first came to the post office. Some of you have lived in this area for many years and may remember them deliver this route: Kee Peterson delivered for Route 1 for thirty-five years, Roy Ketcher delivered for Route 2, and Bob Walton delivered for Route

3. Roy and Bob had been clerks before they started delivering mail. They all retired in 1988.

I was Roy's sub at first. The last ten months, I worked his route six days a week, as he used up his sick leave. He was dying of cancer. I went over to his house, one day, to get his US postal sign for the top of my vehicle. As I was in his garage, he decided to extract payment for the sign and stole a kiss. I told him that I would tell his wife. I was thirty-six, and he was sixty-two. I assume that night he had one less item on his bucket list.

Roy passed away in 1989 at the age of sixty-three. Kee passed away in 2006. Bob, a very sweet man, I do not know if he is still living. I will always cherish them in my heart and be grateful for all they taught me. They were my friends.

The three routes still had wooden cases when I started, but that changed about a year later to metal-slotted rows. I remember how hard it was for the guys to adjust to the change with the names underneath instead of above. They all drove their own cars, and *all* the mail was sorted raw each morning. They strapped out with blue straps, which I continued to use until about a year ago. Now the carriers use tubs or trays. I switched to trays.

In the 1980s, there were more clerks in the office than carriers. As the post office grew, we eventually had five and a half routes and began to deliver out of postal trucks. I was the last to change after delivering mail out of my own vehicle for twenty-six years. I preferred my AWD Subaru and having heat, but that made it hard for my subs, as they were required to have their own vehicle then also. The PO never paid enough to maintain a vehicle, so the repairs came out of your own pocket. I eventually gave in and took a truck four and a half years ago. Just a note—in all of these years, I have never hit a mailbox, delivering mail, and I have always driven a white vehicle. I was bitten by a dog only once.

The mail eventually began to be sorted more and more by machines, which eliminated the clerk's work. In 2005, Maple Plain began to get DPS. That is 95 percent of the letters in delivery point sequence. It made it easier to train the subs and is quite efficient at getting the mail in the right place—well, most of the time. As long as you are dealing with human beings, there will always be mistakes. But considering that each carrier is handling 2,500–5,000 pieces of mail each day, most carriers try hard to be accurate.

I do deeply apologize for all the errors I have made throughout the years. I do hope that you will forgive me.

Since I began in 1984, there have been seven postmasters and numerous OICs. That would be officers in charge. That is not an easy job. The rural carrier position is the best job in the PO (in my opinion). At least it has been for me. I have always loved my job and have been grateful for it. It has changed my life. I have been very blessed. One should always like what they do.

I have watched many of your homes being built and the neighborhoods change throughout the years. The trees have grown so much. I love the beauty of nature and have so much enjoyed all of the aesthetic beauty of your landscapings. There are so many places of quiet serenity and peace. Thank you! You are blessed, and you have blessed me. I have watched many of your children grow into adults with children of their own.

My children have too. I have four—a daughter and three sons. And now, I have eight grandchildren. Children are a gift greater than any words could express. Life is precious.

Friendship is a wonderful gift also. I have made many friends throughout the years. I am so very blessed. You have made my life so much richer and fuller by the kindness and friendship that you have extended to me. Thank you. If I have learned one thing from this job, it is—people are important. You are important. Your life is of great value to those around you, whether they are family, neighbor, or some stranger you meet. You are important, and what you do and what you say will make a difference.

I would like to end this with my three favorite stories.

Many years back, there was a family who lived on Lake Sarah Rd, who had four boys. Now little boys are full of mischief and fun. One day, as I approached their box, I heard giggling in the bushes behind the mailbox. I knew they were up to no good, so I was not surprised when I opened the box to find a little snake. I smiled and said, "Well, hi there, little snake. How are you today?" I'm sure I greatly disappointed those boys that day by not screaming, but it made me smile, and I will never forget them.

Five or so years back, several people on S Lake Sarah Drive were having trouble that summer with mice getting into their mailboxes. There were many shredded documents that season and, I am sure, much frustration. Late in the fall one day, I opened a box to a busy little fellow. He hid under all the shreds, and I just put the mail in and went on my way. These people tended not to get their mail every day, so for three days, he continued to chew. At the end of it all, he finished working on his new home and decided to stake his claim.

That day, as I opened the box, he sat in the middle of his nest triumphantly, like a king who had conquered a new territory, and just looked at me as if to say, "Mine!" I actually sat there for several minutes, and we just watched each other. What I would have given to have a camera that day! It would have been a classic photo. That was the last day of his little life. I was truly sorry the next day, when there was no evidence left of him. If only he had known that life was not that easy.

The last story I would like to share is about Amelia Colburn. She lived on Lake Rebecca Rd. She and her late husband built their retirement home in 1960. He had been a dentist in St. Paul. It was about the time that the park district had decided what land they were going to acquire for the park. Daniel Colburn was not happy about them deciding that his retirement home was going to become a park. He tried to fight them in court but died of a heart attack from the stress.

Amelia was a tiny, little woman, but what she lacked in stature, she made up for in spunk. Theirs was the last home on the road, and she was not going to leave easily. She watched as the park burned down all of her neighbor's homes. Up until the last few years of her life (which were twenty-five years after Daniel had died), she shoveled her very long driveway by hand by herself, grew white daisies in her grass, and drove a red Mustang convertible with wooden blocks on the pedals so she could reach them. She was quick mentally and did her daily crossword puzzles out of the newspaper. She loved to paint flowers and feed the birds. She would get mad at the squirrels for eating the bird seed and shoot them.

One day, she realized that, though she had killed the squirrel, she had forgotten to open the window and had shot through it! That was the day she put her gun away. The last two years of her life, we put her mailbox up by her porch. One day, she did not get her mail out, and as I watched out for her, I went to the door. She seemed ill, and I asked if she needed a doctor. She replied that her son would be there that weekend. I stopped the next day. She was slower to answer, and we went through the same conversation. I told her I would stop again the next day. That was good because, the next day, she didn't answer the door but had left it unlocked. I walked in to find her on the floor. She had been there several hours and had not eaten in two days. She would not let me call the doctor, so I waited there with her for two hours until her daughter came. Amelia was afraid to leave her home. She didn't want the park to win. She passed away, four months later, of congestive heart failure. Her grandson came to live with her, and she died at home. I bought the house from the park and moved it five miles north. My daughter lives in it now. I wish I had told Amelia that I was going to try and save her home. She would have liked that.

I have made many friends throughout the years. Some are still here, some have moved away, and some have passed on. I hope with all my heart that you are blessed, that you know how special you are and how grateful I am that our lives have been connected in some way. I pray that you would know that God loves you very, very much.

As for me, I now will have more time to spend with my family, who I love so much. I will travel, garden, and quilt more, and I love to write, so maybe a book? I know I will enjoy all the blessings God has so generously given to me. He is good!

And may it always be said of Route 1 in Maple Plain that "neither snow nor rain nor heat nor gloom of night stays these carriers from the swift completion of their appointed rounds!" Amen.

—your mail carrier

Christmas Letter 2011

The moment I have been dreading for so long has finally come. It certainly isn't that I am unique, for many have been there before me. Yet as with most things in life, it feels more real, when it has happened to you. And after the moment had passed, I didn't feel any different. I smiled inside because I was still the same, only now I was sixty.

How did this happen? It was only yesterday when I was in my twenties. They say memories are photographs taken with the heart. That must be why I can still see it so clearly. In my twenties, I received five precious gifts. Gifts that changed my life forever. Good gifts are things that last. You never forget, and you never stop cherishing or holding them close to your heart. Never. They are eternal. Forever. And only if the stars broke covenant with the sky would you stop loving them. Not in my lifetime, until my final breath, and on into eternity.

How very blessed I am to have my four children! Each unique and gifted and strong and blessed, and I couldn't be more thankful and filled with gratitude for these treasures. It is all beyond anything words could ever express. I love being a mom. Love. My thirties brought a new adventure. Freedom. Freedom to find who I was.

It was an amazing thing to me to learn that I had choices. I made some—some good and some bad. All things work together for good to those who love God. I believe that. I looked for the good in everything. I wasn't wrong. It isn't because I wanted to believe it to be true but because God said it, and he never lies. Even my failures and disappointments and sorrows have somehow turned around. Only God could do that. It all makes me smile.

My forties were a time of adventure and exploration. I loved traveling. I went everywhere I could. The beauty of nature is breathtaking. I learned that I love the mountains and the streams that sing and dance as they travel over the rocks. I learned that when the problems of life seemed overwhelming, the solution is not to try and remove the rocks but, rather, raise the water. It makes all the difference.

My fifties were a time I learned to let go and rest in God's everlasting arms. I couldn't carry it all. I wasn't created to. Let change happen. There are things bigger than you and me. With God's help, we faced fears and found strength and peace and a contentment I had never walked in before. Every place that I had to let go of was amazingly filled with abundance and wonder and blessings—greater than I could have imagined.

I have a plaque that reads, "Determination—with tenacity, one flourishes in the face of adversity." I like that. It is a signpost to me. The Bible says it another way. It says that Abraham persevered as one who sees him, who is invisible. I love life. My heart is smiling. I love the journey. I want to savor each day, wait to see what each morning brings. May each morning bring us word of his unfailing love.

We are wired to love beauty, adventure, and romance. I don't want to miss a moment of it. I never have. I am very excited about where I am going to. It will be far beyond my wildest imaginations. Until then, I will wait patiently. Patience gives us the ability to embrace and enjoy today. Let us hold it close to our hearts.

I have been thinking a lot about gifts lately. Few gifts bought with money last long. The ability to value something and remember the giver is far greater.

All I have left of my childhood is my little, red Bible, which my grandmother gave to me when I was seven, and my teddy bear. They are both raggedy. I cherish them and still feel loved when I think of them.

Far transcending any gift I have ever received are the people in my life. At sixty, I now see things differently than I did when I was younger. There is not a person in my life that is here by accident. There are no incidentals in my life. I have been placed here to walk with you for a little while. You are not mine, not even my children are. You came from the heart of my Father, loved before the foundation of the world, created and fashioned out of his love. Perfect. Timely.

And the gift that he gave to me was time with you and the privilege of putting into words a small reflection of his heart toward you. He is the best gift, by far, I have ever had the privilege of receiving.

Christmas 2013

I love stories—most of us do. It is why we read books and watch movies and dream. Somewhere in the plot and action, we find a longing we identify with, something our hearts need and search for, whether we are aware of it or not.

We all love adventure, danger, and beauty of some sort—and romance too. Without these things, the entertainment business would not exist. The danger lies in trying to live our lives through the lives of others so much that we could miss our own.

I read a book many years ago called *the Sacred Romance* (a book I strongly recommend). We all live out a story, and each of our stories is of immeasurable value and worth because that is who we are. Our lives are lived out one day at a time and can be easily discarded as unimportant, yet in the bigger picture, they speak volumes to the lives of those around us. We are a masterpiece in the making. Each and every life is of great value.

I have learned, this year, to wait until the story is over before you try and tell it. And I have learned that there are footprints in our lives that we could easily miss if we are not paying attention. They are keys to unlocking the mystery of who we are and what our purpose is in the greater scheme of life.

You are important and greatly loved—when we get this, everything changes.

There are things in our lives that only God can show us. *Truth*—that opens up our eyes to a different view of ourselves and others.

When I was young, I had dreams of what life would be like and what I wanted. There have been some disappointments along the way. We all have them. But as I have pressed on, I have found an increasing strength and patience and a different view of my purpose here in this life.

As I look back over the journey I have traveled so far, I have no regrets, and there is a contentment and peace I never had in my earlier years. The very things I thought were what I really needed have been forgotten and replaced with something better.

I did some scrapbooking and collaging of my early childhood recently. I found a footprint I didn't know existed. My view has been altered. I never really let myself look at my younger years before. I discovered that when our house burned down when I was six, my mom had gone back into the house, after the fire started, and rescued our pictures and baby books and my teddy bear.

I realized that the pictures show that my mom had taken good care of us when we were young, and God has her go back inside that day so he could prove to me—something I just couldn't remember on my own. I see my mom differently now.

This year has brought with it many things for which I am extremely thankful for. After believing Larry's brother would die of stage four cancer, he is in remission and enjoying a second chance at life. My youngest son Mark has come home safely from Afghanistan. Matthew and Stacy were able to move into a new home (a story in itself).

Larry and I took a three-and-a-half-week trip this spring, drove 7,000 miles and touched fourteen states. We got to spend time with my brother's children and their mom. I have a new sister again. (Yeah!) We had such a good time with them!

We had a family reunion, after twenty years or so, with my dad's family. It was good to see them again.

I got new furniture and Larry got a new big-screen TV. Michael and family are doing well, and Michelle got a new job! Larry is adjusting to life with one lung, and he has started a part-time job, delivering pizzas. (He has a lot of energy to work off.) He and I are doing great.

I had to put my mom into a nursing home this fall. That was very hard, but we are taking one day at a time. This May will be my thirty years at the post office. I have one more year to go. (My choice—the new furniture is worth it.)

We truly wish you all great joy, peace, and love. Each of you are very special and greatly loved by God and us. Our lives would not be the same without you!

Christmas 2014

This time of year, I think a lot about giving gifts. I suppose many people do. Actually, I have been thinking a lot about them all year long.

A year ago, I spent some time going back into my early childhood. I discovered that the raggedy teddy bear in my possession was a gift from my grandmother on my very first Christmas. I don't know which is the greater gift—the teddy bear or knowing where it came from. Then there is the little, red Bible my other grandmother gave me on my seventh birthday. I cherish these things.

God is the giver of good gifts—and his last some, forever. Actually, he is a lavish giver. On May 8, I received the gift of a new granddaughter. She came on my mother's birthday. She was early and under three pounds. Eleven days later after she arrived, my mom left. But she left me with a priceless gift that has changed my life. It was the kind that only God can give.

Sometimes, the greatest gift God gives us is just to open our eyes so we can see him and what he has done. We are so blind to many things. He offers us sight.

I have been preparing for retirement the end of the year. I can't do that without remembering with deep gratitude how God gave me my job to begin with. I remember a short, whispered prayer that was shared only with God that, if I ever needed to work, I would like to work at the post office. That was almost thirty-one years ago. The details are too long, but within two months of that prayer, I was offered a job without, even applying.

God heard me. Not only have I been exceedingly blessed all these years but it will extend into retirement and the rest of my life. God's gifts are forever.

Psalm 37:18 says, "The Lord watches over the blameless all their days, and their inheritance will last forever." Now, no one is blameless, but the great gift we celebrate this time of year is the offer of forgiveness through Jesus. When we take that gift and receive God's love and forgiveness, he sees us as blameless. It is a forever gift.

If I have anything to say this year, it is that God sees you and hears you. If you receive the gift that he offers all of us, you will know that he is the only God, and he offers love and compassion and a hope that will last a lifetime, far into the future, and that would be forever.

John 3:16–17 reads:

> For God so loved the world [you] that He gave His only begotten Son that whosoever believes in Him shall not perish, but have everlasting life. For God did not send his Son into the world to condemn the world, but that the world might be saved through Him.

Christmas 2015

Greetings to all of our beloved friends and family this Christmas season! Grace, peace, and joy to you all!

When I was young and in school, my least favorite subject was history. I am not sure why. Maybe because I had this subject during the most stressful year of my childhood—the year my family broke apart—or maybe I just liked math and English better.

Now that I am part of the JOY group at church (Just Older Youth), I have come to understand the value in the story of our lives and how understanding the lessons God is teaching us about how his faithful love will carry us through the greatest storms with quiet assurance.

My favorite scripture is Zephaniah 3:17 (NIV). "The Lord your God is with you. He is mighty to save. He will take great delight in you. He will quiet you with His love. He will rejoice over you with singing."

We took a trip this fall to Williamsburg, Virginia. It was a trip all about history. I was overwhelmed as we toured old churches, plantations, and the city of Old Williamsburg. We visited Jamestown and Mount Vernon. We saw how the colonists lived and died and the struggles they faced in the new world, as they pursued and hoped for a better life. Some had faith in God; others were there just to pursue wealth. As many as 85 percent of them died the first year.

We traveled up to Washington, D.C. It was with great solemnity that we visited Arlington Cemetery and the Vietnam Wall. That was my generation. You cannot help but weep as you view countless names of those who have given their lives for freedom. They can be counted though because each life has value and a story to tell. One could spend a lifetime giving them the attention they deserve.

I have three sons. When I was young, I was afraid to have sons because I was afraid of them being called to war. I would never willingly give my sons to die for another. My youngest son has gone to war now, twice. There are no words to tell how grateful I am that he came home safely. Others have not been so fortunate. I can't imagine.

But as we approach this Christmas season, I cannot help but think about the fact that God loved us so much that, when we were his enemies and were hostile toward him, he chose to willingly give his only beloved son to give his life. Don't miss this—he *willingly* died. He didn't come, hoping he would not die. He came for the express purpose of giving his life for his enemies.

It was and is the greatest gift of love of all time—the gift of life, of hope, of peace, of acceptance, of protection, of provision, of joy to all the world.

There is no other religion in all the world where a God would sacrifice himself out of such great eternal love for mankind. Romans 5:8 reads, "But God demonstrates His own love for us, in that while we were yet sinners, Christ dies for us."

Christmas 2017

Greetings to all those I love!

I have been pondering and waiting to see if there was a Christmas letter in my heart this year, needing to be told. This morning, I realized that there is! It will start with a very unusual scripture out of the book of Hosea. The verses read as such: "Therefore, I will allure her and bring her into the wilderness and speak kindly to her. And there I will give her her vineyards and make the Valley of Achor a door of hope." It is an unusual story yet vaguely familiar. It is the story of love.

Let me tell you about what I found in these words written so long ago.

The word *behold* appears to be a filler word—insignificant, unnecessary, one to gloss over quickly to get to the rest of the story but don't miss it!

If you ponder it for a moment, you have heard it before. It means "to observe with care, gaze upon what I am going to show you!" Look! This is remarkable! Impressive! More wonderful than you ever dreamed or imagined.

We have heard the word *behold* before! The prophets used it many years ago. They said, "Behold, the virgin shall conceive and bear a son, and they shall call his name Immanuel!" (Isaiah 7:14 ESV) (which means "God with us"), and again, the angels said to the shepherds, "Behold, I bring you good tidings of great joy. For unto you is born—a Savior, which is Christ the Lord" (Luke 2:10–11 KJV).

Let's get back to Hosea! "I will allure her and bring her into the wilderness." To allure is the quality of being powerfully and mysteriously attractive. That is what God is! To know him is like a powerful magnet that pulls on our heart's strings.

I have found many things pulling on my heart throughout the years. But God has proved himself to be the unfailing and fierce love that I cannot escape. Nor do I ever want to! His love is so fierce that he must show himself—he must!

Even if we must go into the wilderness (an uninhabitable and hostile place in which few would willingly choose to go yet a necessary place because we are so easily distracted), he has things to say and show us! It is the power of unfailing love, not ours but his!

We are loved! You are loved! He is the love that our hearts crave!

So we find ourselves in the wilderness, and there he speaks kindly to us—tenderly, gently. We are surprised beyond words. Life is hard, painful, hopeless. Our dreams have been shattered, and our future appears beyond repair. We have come to believe we have gone too far. We believe in our worst fears. No one sees us or hears us—alone in the wilderness with unimaginable pain. But in the distance, if we strain our ears, there is a voice—a lovely one, gentle, unimaginable. Are you talking to me?

Can you hear it? He calls us by name—news of great joy! And there, he will give her, her vineyards and make the Valley of Achor a door of hope! One must look intensely at the story of the valley of Achor. It is a place of death. It is a place where one man's sin brought death to his whole family. It is a shocking story—not one we want to think about.

Death is a forever issue, an end to something we have known. Many of us fear death—our own or of those we love. I have feared death that is, but when I whispered my fears to my Father in heaven, he said, "I've got this! Don't be afraid!"

He was true to his word. He held my hand through five deaths this year—deaths of those I have deeply loved! His rod and his staff comforted me. He prepared a table before me. That is what my God does! Amazing! He brings peace and joy in the midst of pain and loss!

The Valley of Achor was repeated in history—it is the story of Jesus! It is a powerful story of God's great, fierce love to turn the table on sin and death and announce that there is a door of hope. He offers us a future and a hope!

It started with a little baby born in a manger by a young virgin and the angels announcing, "Behold, I bring you good news of great joy that will be for all people—a Savior, Christ the Lord!"

Christmas 2018

As I sit here this morning of December 11, 2018, I must admit that my plans were not to write a Christmas letter this year or to even send out many Christmas cards. It is not that I am in a humbug place or my year has ended in an ordinary way, as there is not much to say; quite the contrary, it has been the best year ever!

I just have not had the inspiration to put to words the joy in my heart. And there is great awareness that if there were words to say that would touch one's heart and soul, they would not come from me. Words that touch and change our hearts come from God alone. I am well aware of that. So much to my surprise, the Holy Spirit urged me to get up and write this morning. So here I am. Here we are. I can't help but think that some of the lessons this year has brought are life changers, not just great concepts or wonderful inspiring words.

If one could wrap our hearts around them, if we could see beyond what we have seen in the past, there is a world of wonder, a world of joy, a world of peace, a world of hope, a world of love! It is what the angels came to proclaim to the shepherds, to the world, to you, to me. It is not a Christmas story. It is not fake news. It changes all you have ever known, experienced, or dreamed.

If you search down deep into your soul, your heart, your deepest being and find the greatest longings and dreams, what you really, really need. The truth is that God put those longings there so you would search for and find him.

I was so shocked when I heard him whisper that to me years ago. It was hard for me to embrace, especially when the world and circumstances were loudly proclaiming something different. There was something seen, telling me forcefully, telling me something different than what the unseen Spirit of God was saying. Can you relate? I would guess you can. So this year, God said and meant it, "Let go of the past!" I found myself wanting to hold on to it because, after all, isn't the past part of who we are? We use it to measure ourselves. It is how we define ourselves, whether patting ourselves on the back or condemning ourselves or measuring ourselves against others.

As humans, our value of ourselves or the lack of it is tangled up in our past. God told me to let it go. I am letting it go. There is resistance all around me everywhere—and Warren. Reminders.

We are letting go. The past is over. If we lay all we are at his feet, when the dust and smoke settle down, there will be things of value. No need to fear. God is the great recorder. His records are accurate. He knows it all. We don't need to carry it around. It weighs too much! There is great joy and peace and freedom when we lay down the past!

Second lesson—I read a book recently, which asked the question, What does God celebrate about you?

I must admit I was stunned that I didn't have a clue. I know he loves me but celebrate? I wouldn't know. There are so many others that I could point to, and I believe God celebrates them, but me—I would rather not think about that. Thank you very much! But God seemed to say to me: either I am going to believe what he thinks, or I will believe what other people think.

He gives us a choice. Hmm! I chose that day. I choose God. That day, he told me what he thought. He sees beauty. He sees the beloved of God. He sees his treasured possession. It is time to see ourselves and others through God's eyes. There is joy and peace and freedom when we look at ourselves through God's eyes.

Final lesson for the year—are you ready?

God is bigger than you could ever imagine. God is more kind than you could ever hope for. God is full of love for you more than you could ever comprehend. God is the source of miracles that break through all our boxes. God is the one who created you, chose you, loves you. He sent the angels that night to declare, "Do not fear! I bring you tidings of great joy! For to you is born this day, in the city of David, a savior, who is Christ the Lord." He wants you to find him.

Merry Christmas!

Christmas 2019

Blessings to all our friends and family!

Our hearts are filled with gratitude for each and every one of you!

As Warren and I are finishing up our first full year together, we are overwhelmed by the kindness of God. The journey of life is a precious gift from our heavenly Father, and because of his great love, we desire to live each day in wonder and delight. He is a good Father, and we are learning that he delights in his children.

This truth is breaking the power that the past has had on us. It is lifting us up above the circumstances in our lives. Fear and woundedness no longer shadow our journey. We are safe in our Father's arms!

As we are getting older and the generation ahead of us is gradually moving into eternity, I have pondered the scripture from 1 Peter 3:9. "For you were called so that you may inherit a blessing" (NIV). Actually, this year, the Lord has been teaching us a lot about the word *inheritance*. I have misunderstood many things about this word.

Psalm 16:5–6 says, "The Lord is the portion of my inheritance and my cup, You have made my lot secure; the boundary lines have fallen for me in pleasant places; surely I have a delightful inheritance."

My heart knows it is true. Yet I imagine that from the view of others. It might not appear to be so. It is true that I have struggled with many questions about my heritage, my family of origin; maybe some of you have as well. The battle in my mind has, at times, stolen my self-worth and deceived me, defining me by my circumstances, the opinions of others, and my feelings. But I am learning the truth. We have been called to inherit a blessing!

Oftentimes, I have defined my *inheritance* as a possible future possession. It only comes with the loss of someone we love, with pain and grief. I have misunderstood. The scriptures are clear. "Surely, I *have* a delightful inheritance."

Because of God's great gift of salvation through Jesus, I have a forever companion and comforter, the Holy Spirit, living inside of me. I have a big brother who goes before me, protecting me, defending me. I have the most loving Father ever, who adores me and cherishes me. I have abundant joy and peace and a future that is bright.

My children and family are part of my inheritance, and what belongs to me, belongs to them. It is a done deal with God. What we inherit as children of God can never be stolen, lost, or grow old. The things of this world do not begin to compare to the treasures we have.

I have been slow to understand what God has given to those who receive his Son, Jesus, those who put their trust in him. But I see him smiling and telling me that he knew all along that I would figure it out, as he takes my hand, encouraging me to walk with him into the future and the wonderful adventures he has in store for all who love him.

CPSIA information can be obtained
at www.ICGtesting.com
Printed in the USA
JSHW030544090323
38673JS00001B/2